HOW LONG, O LORD?

HOPE AND HELP WHEN YOU HAVE BEEN DEEPLY HURT

by

KRISTIN A. VARGAS

CONCORDIA PUBLISHING HOUSE · SAINT LOUIS

Published by Concordia Publishing House
3558 S. Jefferson Avenue, St. Louis, MO 63118–3968
1-800-325-3040 • www.cph.org

Scripture quotations are from the ESV® Bible (The Holy Bible, English Standard Version®), copyright © 2001 by Crossway, a publishing ministry of Good News Publishers. Used by permission. All rights reserved.

Quotations marked *LSB* are from *Lutheran Service Book*, copyright © 2006 Concordia Publishing House. All rights reserved.

Manufactured in the United States of America

Library of Congress Cataloging-in-Publication Data

Names: Vargas, Kristin A., author.

Title: How long, O Lord? : hope and help when you have been deeply hurt / Kristin Vargas.

Description: St. Louis : Concordia Publishing House, 2018. | Includes bibliographical references and index.

Identifiers: LCCN 2017050435 (print) | LCCN 2017057784 (ebook) | ISBN 9780758658654 | ISBN 9780758658647

Subjects: LCSH: Suffering--Religious aspects--Christianity. | Traumatism. | Violence--Religious aspects--Christianity. | Death--Religious aspects--Christianity. | Grace (Theology)

Classification: LCC BV4909 (ebook) | LCC BV4909 .V37 2018 (print) | DDC 241/.697--dc23

LC record available at https://lccn.loc.gov/2017050435

1 2 3 4 5 6 7 8 9 10   27 26 25 24 23 22 21 20 19 18

My soul also is greatly troubled.
But You, O LORD—how long?

Turn, O LORD, deliver my life; save me
for the sake of Your steadfast love.

—*Psalm 6:3–4*

CONTENTS

EDITOR'S PREFACE

ife in a fallen world is often harsh and difficult. The things we experience can cause tremendous suffering and devastate our souls and spirits, making us question God's holiness, love, and power. In the face of severe trauma, spiritual hurt and confusion frequently lasts years, decades, or even a person's entire earthly lifetime. That is why this study is titled *How Long, O Lord?* How long must the pain endure? How long must our questions go unanswered? How long until we are finally whole?

This study looks primarily at traumatic events suffered by military personnel. At times, you will come across intense examples that you may find unsettling. These are not meant to cause you pain but to give you a window into the spiritual trauma suffered by servicemen and women. These examples are also meant to help you understand the similar spiritual trauma suffered by first responders and victims of abuse.

Ultimately, there is only one lasting solution to spiritual damage and pain. Ironically, it, too, was a traumatic event: the crucifixion, suffering, and death of God's own Son, our Lord and Savior, Jesus Christ. But it was through His mortal pain and agony and His victorious resurrection that our sins were removed. It is through Jesus' victory over all that harms us that God offers us hope, courage, peace, and healing for this lifetime. And it is through Christ's ultimate victory, which we will see when He returns to judge the living and the dead, that He will wipe away every tear from our eyes and rid His creation of pain and trauma forever.

"Amen. Come, Lord Jesus!" (Revelation 22:20).

ACKNOWLEDGMENTS

Projects like this are not a one-man show. It took a lot of people to set the stage and enable me to write on a difficult—sometimes distressing—subject.

Much of the information you read here I first encountered as a graduate student, and I am grateful that I can now pass it on to other Christians in churches around the country. In particular, I thank Dr. Rita Nakashima Brock for her work at the Soul Repair Center in Fort Worth, Texas. If not for her week-long intensive seminar that I attended in January 2016, this Bible study would not exist.

Two other professors made a deep impression on this work. Dr. Wil Gafney, Associate Professor of Hebrew Bible at Brite Divinity School, was integral to my learning via her in-depth lectures on the world of the ancient Israelites. The lessons regarding Joshua, Judges, and the prophets all owe a debt to her teaching. I am also indebted to Dr. Charles K. Bellinger, Associate Professor of Theology and Ethics at Brite Divinity School, for introducing me to the world of ethics, religion, and violence. His teaching and mentorship have changed my life and significantly influenced the creation of this study.

Next, I need to thank my church, St. Paul Lutheran of Fort Worth, Texas. If it had not been for the trust and encouragement of Revs. John Messmann, Bud Beverly, Doug Widger, and Martin Danner, I would never have taught the Sunday School series on moral injury that led directly to the making of this book. I thank Jennifer Gross, the coordinator of St. Paul's adult ministry programs, for always seeing that our class had everything it needed, from handouts to chairs. I also will be forever grateful to my gracious audience who participated in that first experimental class.

Thank you to my editor, Rev. Wayne Palmer, and his team at Concordia Publishing House for being my guide and support during this process. Wayne's keen understanding of pastoral care, theology, and the Bible was invaluable in keeping this work doctrinally sound.

Last, I must thank my husband and family for their support and encouragement throughout the process.

INTRODUCTION

first encountered the subject of moral injury in my graduate studies. Extreme trauma shakes or shatters a person's moral expectations, faith, and beliefs. Psychologists and clinicians differentiate this moral damage from the psychological damage called post-traumatic stress disorder (PTSD).

I quickly came to understand that "moral injury" is spiritual brokenness and conflict. A soul-damaging experience can either shake one's faith to the point that one abandons belief in good and God, or strengthen one's faith as the Holy Spirit works through Word and Sacrament to move the believer closer to his or her Creator and Savior.

Moral injury and soul repair is a challenging topic. But understanding it will help the members of your congregation grow in compassion for one another and be better neighbors to one another—especially to those who have worked in occupations with high risks of trauma (e.g., military personnel, first responders, medical personnel, counselors, ministers, and journalists). Moral injury is also quite common among victims of domestic and sexual abuse. For the purposes of this class, I use the military as my default example.

One lesson in this book represents one week in a twelve-week study. This book is intended for a group Bible study, but it can also be read as an individual at one's own pace. The first six lessons of the study establish a basic concept of moral injury alongside biblical examples of spiritual brokenness, desolation, and trauma. Lesson 7 marks a turning point to explore God's pathway to healing, restoration, and reconciliation.

Unless referencing content or stories previously published in print, personal names in this study have been changed to protect the privacy of individuals.

A word about terminology: Many veterans dislike the label *post-traumatic stress disorder*, especially since the symptoms associated with the disorder can be temporary side effects of combat violence. The use of the acronym PTSD, therefore, is more appropriate for those who have suffered for years without treatment. In this book, I will typically use the term *post-traumatic stress* (PTS).

I commend you for your interest in the topic of moral injury and your courage to care enough about the trauma of others. God bless you on your journey through moral injury, being guided by His Word!

Lesson 1

CRISIS OF CONSCIENCE

Today, as a class or an individual, you will embark upon a journey that will take you through the fires of spiritual brokenness caused by violent trauma. This journey will lead you through some of the most challenging and disquieting chapters of the Bible. But before you open your Bible, let us first look at the history, the *why*, and the definition of our topic.

A BRIEF HISTORY

For quite some time, Western culture has been a therapeutic culture. As science has advanced in the last several centuries, the trend in our culture has become to rely on various scientific disciplines to solve our life problems. As new problems have arisen, new scientific fields have developed to solve those problems. Thus, with the turn of the twentieth century, psychology, anthropology, neuroscience, and modern medical philosophy emerged, coinciding with and rising out of the wars of the twentieth century.

When the first veterans of World War I came home (and then the veterans of World War II, Korea, Vietnam, and so on), many were visibly and invisibly broken. Medical and psychiatric care treated their physical and mental ailments, but science could not treat their spiritual injuries. Therefore, their spiritual needs were largely ignored. The dependence on scientific disciplines also resulted in a widespread denial of the spiritual aspect of human existence.

Let me give a few real-life examples from some veterans' experiences. Joseph fought in the Korean War when he was eighteen. He spent one terrible night in a foxhole, holding the hand of his unit mate who died sometime during the night. In the morning, Joseph couldn't pry his hand out of the corpse's as rigor mortis had set in. When he eventually managed to free his hand and return to base, Joseph was not the same man. When he returned to the United States, he was put in a psychiatric ward for quite some time. But despite the efforts of psychiatrists and clinicians, when Joseph was discharged, his wife and children did not recognize the person who returned to them. The trauma of that night in the foxhole and the guilt he feels over the loss of his friend still linger, even after all these years.

This resembles the story of my own grandfather, Wesley. During World War II, he thought he'd managed to carry his wounded buddy out of danger to safety until a German sniper put a bullet in the center of this friend's head, while Wesley cradled him in his arms. My grandfather waited for the sniper to pull the trigger again. He waited and waited. He could almost hear the sniper whisper, "Your life is in my hands. *I* choose whether you live or die." The sniper did not kill him, although he had the opportunity, and that experience haunted my grandfather until his death. "Why was *I* spared and not my friend?" he would ask.

Last is Janet's story. She was a military nurse stationed in Japan during the Vietnam War. During the Tet Offensive, massive casualties flooded her hospital. She vividly remembers the gory sights and deep disturbance the medical staff experienced when there were so many soldiers they could not save. Even the doctors wept. Her return Stateside with her veteran husband did even more damage as the average American did not understand or sympathize with what they had experienced and instead looked with scorn on their involvement in the unpopular war.

In 2009, an article by Brett Litz and a team of authors rocked the clinical psychology community. It described a study conducted by psychologists in conjunction with the U.S. Marine Corps. It admitted that for various reasons, little attention had been paid to the moral and ethical distress servicemen and women face in addition to or alongside PTS symptoms. Astonishingly, the study acknowledged that a new approach involving spiritual communities was needed. The article all but admitted that clinicians had no expertise in this area of human life and needed help from those who did.

WHY THIS MATTERS

The atrociously high suicide rate of veterans suggests our society has failed in its responsibility to return our troops to civilian life. The U.S. Department of Veterans Affairs (VA) recently conducted the most comprehensive study of veteran suicides to date. Published in 2016, the study revealed that twenty veterans commit suicide every day. Many experts think that the actual number is higher since, statistically, veterans' favorite method of suicide is by motorcycle, and it is extremely hard for a coroner to determine if a motorcycle accident is suicide.

Beyond devastating statistics like these, the topic of moral injury is important for Christians because we care about people's lives and quality of life. Each person is created by God and loved by Him. Therefore, we want to care for all people who are suffering because God cares about them—no matter who they are.

This is where our secular world falls short. But this is where the Church can shine. As sisters and brothers in faith, as priests under our High Priest, Jesus Christ, we are being asked for help. We can share with others the spiritual healing that Jesus gives. This is the *why* and the purpose of this Bible study: to prepare us for spiritual care for those suffering from the aftereffects of violence on the human soul or spirit.

DEFINITION OF THE TERM

Experts and academics use the term *moral injury* to describe the distress that results from human beings committing, seeing, or experiencing acts that go against their beliefs of what is morally right and wrong. Moral injury is a crisis of conscience. It is damage to the soul. When a person suffers this kind of damage, his entire belief system and his understanding of good and evil are altered or destroyed. The trauma that caused this disruption changes a person, no longer allowing him or her to see the world as he or she once did. Such a person often feels betrayed: by God, by a superior commander, by a nation, or by loved ones.

For the purposes of this Bible study, active duty and veteran military servicemen and women will be the primary sources of illustrations of our topic, but this kind of spirit-rending damage is by no means restricted to military servicepeople.

Violent trauma and the destruction it wreaks on the human spirit can come to any one of us at any time in our lives. Pilots, first responders, EMTs (emergency medical technicians), firefighters, emergency staff in hospitals, and police officers all tend to experience moral injury. Victims of violent crimes, sexual assault, or child abuse may also deal with this kind of injury. The great unspoken secret of many women who have had abortions is the psychological and moral wounds they quietly endure, leaving their families in ignorance of their pain, remaining alone in dealing with these experiences.

THE SHEDDING OF BLOOD IN THE BIBLE

Moral injury harms us because God requires us in the Fifth Commandment to respect human life. Why? At the very beginning of the Bible, we read, "God created man in His own image, in the image of God He created him; male and female He created them" (Genesis 1:27). Of course, shortly after Adam and Eve were created, they rebelled against God, ate the forbidden fruit, and became sinners. God commands us to respect human life because we are His image-bearers and the prohibition against taking life is written into our hearts by natural law.

But the Bible seems to show a contradiction here. Often we see God condoning killing—even commanding it—especially in war. This is when it is helpful to do a short word study in the Bible's original languages. The Hebrew Old Testament uses more than one word for our word *kill* in English. The term used in the Fifth Commandment, *ratsakh,* is never used for the killing of animals and plants, for self-defense, or in the context of warfare. Instead, *ratsakh* means the shedding of innocent human blood either intentionally (murder) or negligently (manslaughter).

In light of what God says about the importance of our respect for human life because we are His image-bearers, it is easy to see how killing in the line of duty or in the heat of battle can damage the spirit, even though those actions technically do not violate the Fifth Commandment.

READING FOR THE WEEK

Read and contemplate Lamentations 3 this week. Churches have used this chapter in worship to address the moral injury of veterans returning to civilian life. Jeremiah's words speak to the hearts and minds of victims of moral injury. Read through the chapter several times, both as one who may have suffered moral injury and as one caring for others within a local church.

DISCUSSION QUESTIONS

1. Can you think of anyone in your personal history who was touched by moral injury?

2. Who else besides those who have witnessed or participated in combat and warfare could be at risk for spiritual trauma caused by violence?

3. Why do you think the rise of scientific knowledge undermined the general belief in humans' spiritual nature?

4. What does it mean to be an image-bearer of God? In other words, what qualities do we as human beings exhibit in our nature that reflect our Creator?

Lesson 2

BODY AND SOUL

I n today's lesson, we will consider the physical side of moral injury in how the brain responds to trauma as well as scientific insight on moral development. We will then discuss the Bible's view of the spiritual aspects of human beings, including the soul, heart, and spirit. We will describe the interaction and distinction between PTS and moral injury. Then we will consider the power of trauma in human memory.

In the Bible lesson, we will study the Book of Joshua and consider his account through the lens of trauma and moral injury.

OUR BRAINS

Neuroscience research provides a wealth of information to help us understand how God has designed our brains. In order to understand the havoc that violent trauma causes for a human being, we must briefly examine this field of science.

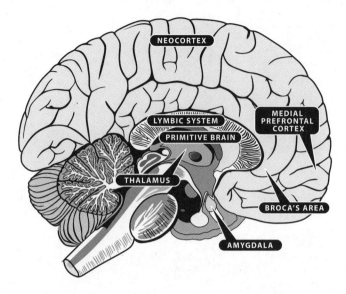

There are three areas in our brains that interact with one another and control our bodies: the primitive brain, the limbic system, and the neocortex.

The primitive brain is always active; it keeps us breathing, our heart beating, our muscles functioning, and our other systems running automatically, even when we are sleeping. Importantly, this is also the seat of self-preservation and aggression. It is the first part of a baby's brain to develop in a mother's womb.

The limbic system is the middle part of our brain where our emotions are produced. During the first two years of life, this part of the brain is actively forming; a child's early life experiences shape this part of the brain, creating for the baby a framework within which to view and understand the world. Every emotion—joy, fear, anger, sorrow—comes from here, along with emotionally charged memories. There is a specific structure called the amygdala in this part of the brain. The amygdala controls our body's response to danger, like a home's security alarm system. The primitive brain and the limbic system work together in an intricate dance to give us the emotions we experience.

The third main part of our brain is the neocortex, also known as the rational brain. The neocortex is uniquely developed in human beings. It is the seat of our intellect, abstract thought, spatial awareness, and creativity. It is also the section that controls speech, specifically a spot called Broca's area. Under normal circumstances, the left and right hemispheres of the brain, where the three main parts of the brain are located, communicate beautifully so that we can perceive and comprehend the world around us.

Neural pathways allow these different parts of the brain to interact. For example, if something startles us, the amygdala (our alarm) is triggered; it then sends a message down to the hypothalamus to turn on the body's stress hormone system and the autonomic nervous system. The nervous system sends nerve impulses throughout the body to ready us for flight or fight. This is when our blood pressure soars, our heart starts to pound, and our oxygen intake increases as we breathe faster.

If the threat that gave us a fright turns out to be harmless—the sound of a car backfiring, for instance—the neocortex allows us to calm down. It does this through the medial prefrontal cortex, which is located above our eyes. This part of the brain is like the police officer who responds to the house alarm. If it is a false alarm, the medial prefrontal cortex will override the alarm and allow the body to go back into a state of rest.

What happens to the intricate dance of the three parts of the brain when an unprecedented, traumatic event happens? The alarm goes off, but if something is preventing the fight-or-flight reaction, such as if a person is being held down and tortured, assaulted, raped, or kidnapped, then the body will stay in a heightened alarm state. Sometimes the person will freeze or collapse, and when the event is over, that heightened alarm state does not go away. The neocortex will not function as it was designed to because the emotional brain has taken over.

When something triggers a memory of the traumatic event, the emotional brain causes the person to relive the event again, since the rational brain is not functioning the way it should anymore. That person is stuck in a terrible hyperawareness or, alternatively, if the neocortex takes over and suppresses the limbic system, an unbreakable numbness. This disruption of the normal brain processes creates a terrible strain on the body in the long run, potentially causing a wide range of health problems such as chronic fatigue, fibromyalgia, and a variety of autoimmune diseases.

HOW WE DEVELOP MORALITY

Neurons are extremely important messengers within our brains. Not long ago, neurologists discovered special kinds of neurons called mirror neurons. These neurons were so named because they enable human beings to start to mirror parents and caregivers from birth. This is an unconscious activity. Because imitating the behavior that is modeled for us is as natural as breathing, scientists believe this is how we learn right from wrong at the deepest, most basic level.

Just as the interactions between our rational and emotional brains can be disrupted by trauma, so also our mirroring instincts can be affected by trauma. This can severely impact our ability to trust others and relate to them, often producing feelings of isolation.

THE HEART AND SOUL

"Man does not live by bread alone" (Deuteronomy 8:3). We are more than just physical beings being run as biological machines. Now that we understand a few basics about our physical nature, what can we say about something as mysterious as the human soul? Professor of neurosurgery Michael Egnor shares a trade secret in his article "A Map of the Soul" in *First Things* magazine. Many neurosurgeons see things in surgery that can't be explained. He and others in his field see firsthand that the mind and the brain are different and that intellect and will belong to the immaterial world. The best explanation for this, he discovered, was in the writings of Thomas Aquinas. Not everything about the human being can be explained by cells, atoms, and brain matter.

The ancient Greek philosophers believed that the human being was made up of two parts: body and soul. The Bible refers to three parts: body, soul, and spirit (literally "the breath of life"). In the Bible, the soul is often used to refer to a whole human being as well as to a human being's relationship to self, others, and the Creator. To Aquinas and Egnor, therefore, the soul is the seat of the mind.

Yet, there is a fourth aspect of our humanity to contemplate. There are many Bible verses that talk about soul and spirit, but when we look at the *moral* experience of the human being, the Bible points us to the heart. In the Old Testament, there is a famous passage in Deuteronomy, which Jesus calls the first of the two greatest commandments: "You shall love the LORD your God with all your heart and with all your soul and with all your might" (Deuteronomy 6:5).

The prophet Ezekiel, speaking on God's behalf, describes the heart as a conduit of both good and evil:

> And I will give them one heart, and a new spirit I will put within them. I will remove the heart of stone from their flesh and give them a heart of flesh, that they may walk in My statutes and keep My rules and obey them. And they shall be My people, and I will be their God. But as for those whose heart goes after their detestable things and their abominations, I will bring their deeds upon their own heads, declares the Lord GOD. (Ezekiel 11:19–21)

Jesus emphasized the attitude of the heart in the Sermon on the Mount as He expanded upon the meaning of the Commandments. Likewise James instructed early Christians, "Draw near to God, and He will draw near to you. Cleanse your hands, you sinners, and purify your hearts, you double-minded" (James 4:8).

Our bodily, psychological, and spiritual natures are intrinsically tied together; this is why our mental state can affect our physical state and vice versa. Our spiritual state will also affect our mental and physical well-being. This is why laughter *can* be the best medicine or why losing the will to live can send someone into death, even when medical experts believe a person will recover. As Proverbs says, "A joyful heart is good medicine, but a crushed spirit dries up the bones" (Proverbs 17:22).

THE RELATIONSHIP BETWEEN PTS AND MORAL INJURY

In light of our reflections on the complexities of the various aspects of a human person, it is vital to understand as we continue through this Bible study that PTS is *not* the same as moral injury. PTS is a physical phenomenon. Brain scans of PTS sufferers show that the neocortices in their brains have shrunk. This physical damage is not necessarily permanent. The brain is a muscle, and muscles can atrophy if they aren't fully used. Medicine, therapy, and sometimes just sleep can help the neocortex return to its ordinary size.

In the case of PTS, the primitive brain and the limbic system are in overdrive, constantly creating heightened awareness for the task of self-preservation. The rational brain is being used less, and therefore it has less control over the fear, anger, and aggression being produced by the other two parts of the brain.

Moral injury is caused by the disruption of one's belief system. We can see an example in the well-known Holocaust survivor, writer, and Nobel Laureate, Elie Wiesel (1928–2016). A prisoner in the Auschwitz and Buchenwald concentration camps, Wiesel was orphaned at age 16 and lost most of his family. It took him ten years to decide to write about his experiences. In his autobiographical book, *Night*, Wiesel wrote of the day he lost his faith in God. He spent the rest of his life trying to bring meaning back into the lives of those who experienced the Holocaust. Wiesel died an agnostic, never returning to the Jewish faith exemplified by his mother.

Another example of moral injury comes from the Vietnam War. A virtue ethic was instilled in soldiers during basic training, a code of conduct that signified fighting with honor. But the realities of combat often seemed to conflict with that code. The dissonance caused by having to kill a child who held a grenade, for example, eroded soldiers' sense of honor and goodness to the point that many felt unclean or evil—the perpetrators of violence instead of heroic saviors.

PTS and moral injury are different, but they can go hand in hand and can share certain similarities. Below is a table to demonstrate the main differences between them. Notice how PTS causes primarily physiological problems, while moral injury causes negative emotional responses:

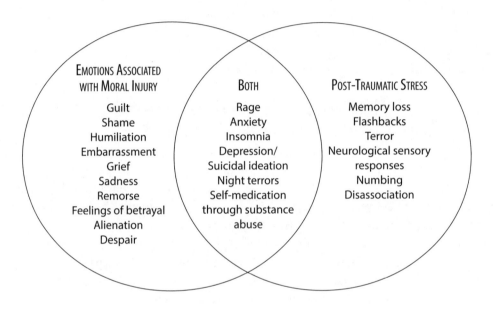

EMOTIONS ASSOCIATED WITH MORAL INJURY

Guilt
Shame
Humiliation
Embarrassment
Grief
Sadness
Remorse
Feelings of betrayal
Alienation
Despair

BOTH

Rage
Anxiety
Insomnia
Depression/
Suicidal ideation
Night terrors
Self-medication
through substance
abuse

POST-TRAUMATIC STRESS

Memory loss
Flashbacks
Terror
Neurological sensory
responses
Numbing
Disassociation

TRAUMA AND MEMORY

Although specialists' theories differ concerning how memory loss works, memory loss is an often-reported phenomenon among those who experience traumas such as natural disasters, accidents, war violence, kidnapping, torture, concentration camps, physical abuse, and sexual abuse. However, lost memories can be recovered. And when they are, it is as if the brain had been storing the memory in the subconscious, for recovered memories are just as accurate as memories that were never lost.

Traumatic memories are different from normal memories. In a normal memory, such as from one's wedding day, the details might become vague and blurred by the passing of time, but one can still remember getting up that day, getting dressed, arriving at the venue, walking down the aisle, and cutting the cake in a chronological timeline.

By contrast, traumatic memories can become detached from the original circumstances in which they happened. When this happens, the part of the rational brain that tracks time is not working correctly. This is called disassociation. The result is that disturbing recollections of the event can become as vivid as if the person were experiencing the event all over again, causing overwhelming emotional reactions and physical reactions such as nausea and dizziness. Brodmann's area 19, which controls the processing of images we see, can also be activated at random times and cause a person to relive a traumatizing event as if it was happening all over again. This is what is happening in the case of a flashback. Another possible effect of a traumatic memory is dumbfounding. The area of the rational brain that controls speech, Broca's area, can shut down because of trauma, making it impossible for a person to speak or to speak about the traumatic event.

These phenomena make listening well very important when interacting with those suffering from moral injury. Listening to someone's story means putting aside the natural inclination to interject yourself into a story or to correct elements of a story that a person describes as happening right now when you know they happened in the past. It is important to let a trauma survivor tell the story the way he or she wants to, even if that story changes slightly with every telling. It is especially imperative to avoid accusing a trauma survivor of lying because of these seemingly inconsistent accounts. The trauma survivor is trying to put together the jigsaw puzzle of a memory so that he or she can place that event in perspective and put it safely in the past. In a way, a person who has lost then recalled a traumatic memory re-creates the memory by telling his story again and again. Human beings ascribe meanings to memories. The repetition of recalling a memory can desensitize the brain to the memory and help train the brain to assign a constructive meaning to that memory. This is part of the healing process. In a later lesson, we will describe ways that you can practice listening well to veterans who need to share their stories.

JOSHUA AND WAR IN THE BIBLE

The sobering truth is that violence is never innocuous. Those of us who have not experienced warfare or moral injury may forget this sometimes. We may be tempted to read stories of warfare in the Bible, even warfare that was carried out according to God's command like the military campaigns of Joshua, and be excited by the thrill of the battle. But studying moral injury helps us realize that in the messy, complicated, corrupt world we live in, even a holy war like the one Joshua fought did not come without traumatic ramifications for those involved. When we realize how much the people in the Bible are just like us, we realize that being God's people does not necessarily protect us from pain and difficulty in this life.

WHY BODY AND SOUL BELONG TOGETHER

Moral injury happens to human beings when they see or experience events that undo the union of their own or other people's bodies and souls. The Bible's witness that God created us not only as bodies but also with souls means that God never intended our bodies and souls to be separated or to function independently from one another. Or said in another way, God never intended His creation to be severed and razed by death and evil. Seeing violence done to a human being—a body-soul creation of God—is never what God intended for us to experience. Being violated in either body or soul by violence or abuse done to us is never what God intended for us, because He created us to be whole in both body and soul.

The ultimate violation of body and soul is death. God cares as much for our bodies as He does for our souls. He created us as a union of both body and soul. So it is the ultimate grieving of His creation when our soul and our body are wrenched apart by our death.

Yet God was not willing to leave us in the severed, torn-apart state that our sin, evil, and death have landed us in. The severing of body and soul in this life and ultimately in our death is not the end of the story. What God once created He will re-create. God the Father will one day finish the re-creating of His creation that He began when He raised His own Son from death to life on Easter. One day, God will unite our body and soul perfectly together—but this time, forever (see 1 Corinthians 15:42–57). As Paul says, "For as by a man came death, by a man has come also the resurrection of the dead. For as in Adam all die, so also in Christ shall all be made alive" (1 Corinthians 15:21–22).

Until then, God still does care for both our bodies and our souls. And the things that cause us moral injury grieve Him deeply, for though He knows the future renewal and new life of His creation, He still loves it and us now. Notice the closing blessing that is given to God's children after they receive Jesus' body and blood in the Lord's Supper: "The body and blood of our Lord Jesus Christ strengthen and preserve you in body and soul to life everlasting. Depart in peace" (LSB, p. 199). God cares about both until and through life everlasting.

READING FOR THE WEEK

During the coming week, read and meditate on Psalm 7.

DISCUSSION QUESTIONS

1. In the lesson, memory is described with the metaphor of a jigsaw puzzle. What are some other ways to conceptualize how memory works?

2. What is the difference between PTS and moral injury? What symptoms do they share?

3. Read Deuteronomy 4:1–4, 9–10; Matthew 11:28–30; Hebrews 4:11–13 concerning what the Bible says about our heart, soul, and spirit. How do these verses affect your understanding of human nature?

4. Moral behavior is developed first through imitating parents and caregivers. Why do you think Paul emphasized imitation in 1 Corinthians 4:16; 11:1; and Philippians 3:17?

Lesson 3

THE FATHERS VS. FREUD

In fourth-century Rome, Ambrose, the Bishop of Milan, publicly barred Emperor Theodosius from receiving Holy Communion. The issue began when the Commandant of Thessalonica was killed in a riot. Emperor Theodosius, known for his temper, was enraged by the news. He sent to Thessalonica a proclamation that the rioters were pardoned. But when some seven thousand people gathered in an arena to celebrate the pardon, Theodosius ordered the army to trap the people inside the arena and kill them. The slaughter did not end until all were dead.

When Bishop Ambrose heard this, he made sure the next time Theodosius went to church in Milan, he would be there to meet Theodosius at the door. The emperor acknowledged that Ambrose was right to call him to repent. He did repent publicly of his sin, and he decreed that no public execution would ever occur without a delay of thirty days.

As we have noted, our therapeutic culture treats the massive damage done to the soul in warfare as something to be fixed through pharmaceuticals and years of therapy. Though we would not deny that those means of support can help a person, Christianity historically has a particular way of treating the troubled soul. Christians and Early Church leaders did not necessarily ban believers from serving in the military. In fact, there have been three views on war held by Christians at different times in history.

THREE CHRISTIAN ATTITUDES CONCERNING THE SWORD

PACIFISM:

There is no justifiable reason to destroy human life. There are many varieties of pacifism. Proponents: Tertullian, Lactantius, the Waldenses, Erasmus, the Swiss Brethren, Mennonites, the Quakers, Leo Tolstoy

JUSTIFIABLE OR "JUST" WAR:

There are some cases when war is justifiable. One can conclude a war is just if at least five of the following conditions are met:

1. *Just cause*—The reason for the war must be just (e.g., defense after an attack).
2. *Legitimate authority*—Only a recognized sovereign nation can declare a just war.
3. *Comparative justice*—The declarer of a just war must have a moral reason that outweighs the justice of maintaining the status quo.
4. *Right intention*—The goal should be the restoration of peace (not a regime change).
5. *Probability of success*—There must be hope of winning the war.
6. *Last resort*—Everything else has been tried.
7. *Proportionality of results*—The expected result must outweigh the cost of war.
8. *Right spirit*—The war is perceived as a tragic necessity.

Proponents: Ambrose, Augustine, Aquinas, Luther, Calvin, Francisco de Vitoria, Francisco Suarez

CRUSADE OR HOLY WAR:

God or His authorities on earth (for Catholics, the Pope) command a war. Proponents: Pope Urban II

Although some early Christian leaders like Lactantius (ca. AD 304) believed God forbade warfare of any kind, other Church leaders wrestled with the idea of a "just" war, which had been proposed by various Greco-Roman thinkers. Athanasius thought that it was wrong to kill in general but praiseworthy to kill an enemy in lawful war. Basil the Great did not consider killing in war to be homicide. St. Augustine, the most famous early proponent of the Just War Theory, did not believe killing in war was a violation of the Fifth Commandment.

Regardless of the multiplicity of views among Early Church leaders about killing in war, the early councils of the Church, including the Council of Nicaea in AD 325, took very seriously that the shedding of blood would inherently have a harmful effect on the bearer of the sword. Returning soldiers underwent a period in which they did not receive Holy Communion. Instead, they were retrained in the Christian faith, becoming like catechumens again, while going through a process of purification. Like Ambrose with Emperor Theodosius, the Church's way of dealing with moral injury involves truthfully stating what proceeds from sin and evil in the world, calling for repentance when a person has contributed to moral injury for others, and then forgiving a person's sins for Jesus' sake and giving that person the purity of a new life in Jesus.

THE RISE OF THE THERAPEUTIC CULTURE

There have been changes in modern warfare as well as modern psychology that have heightened our secular society's awareness of and response to moral injury. Sensitivity to the moral pain of soldiers is actually quite new in the secular world. Until very recently, a soldier's feelings of wrongdoing, guilt, or shame were held in disdain by the public and viewed as bizarre neuroses by psychiatrists. For example, during the American Civil War, the sufferings of soldiers were attributed to homesickness or nostalgia. Russian psychiatrists after the Russo-Japanese War of 1904 and 1905 explained their soldiers' suffering as "organic psychoses."

FREUD AND VETERANS

The most well-known pioneer of modern psychology is Sigmund Freud. Freud also pioneered work with veterans. Before the end of WWI, Freud had written that he expected soldiers to return home and pick up where they had left off. After treating many of the returned veterans, he was shocked and troubled to find that they were far different men than when they had left. He termed the phenomenon he saw "war neurosis." In WWII, it was called "shell shock." After Vietnam, "post-traumatic stress disorder" became the new nomenclature.

Using Freud's research, military physicians as well as independent psychiatrists attempted to abate these symptoms with neglect and electric shock treatments. An extremely negative perception of this "neurosis" took root because its causes were not understood and the field of neurology itself was still in its inception. A soldier who experienced this condition was considered cowardly, mentally deficient, or diseased, and the "cure" was often to break the suffering man's will. Since then, the clinical fields of psychiatry and psychology have made enormous strides in both neurology and pharmacology. However, note the differences between how this suffering has been viewed by the Church and how it has been viewed at various times by our modern therapeutic culture.

Reflexive Fire Training and Battle Readiness

The need to care for the moral injury of soldiers has only multiplied in the twentieth century with developments in military technology. After World War II, U.S. Army historian Brigadier General S. L. A. Marshall published a book that claimed his research revealed that during the war, a mere 25 percent of combat soldiers fired directly at the enemy. In fact, most soldiers would not fire even when their own lives were at stake! He suggested this was true because many of the young men who fought in WWII were raised to believe human life is sacred, and boot camp was not erasing a lifetime of belief. The statistics were so shocking the Army decided to revamp how they trained soldiers to kill. New techniques, such as reflexive fire training, were developed in order to overcome soldiers' inhibitions about taking human lives.

Essentially, soldiers were trained to shoot without thinking, completely bypassing the moral decision-making part of the brain. By the time of the Korean War, the shooting rates rose to at least 50 percent. By the time the Vietnam War was at its height, the rates had risen to between 80 and 90 percent.

Some of the techniques used to disrupt the moral decision-making of soldiers in order to make them more effective combatants were dehumanizing the enemy, commanding to kill outside of the rules of engagement, and driving a soldier into a berserk, rage state. Enemies were called by derogatory names to help soldiers perceive the enemy not as human but rather as animals—killable vermin. A soldier would not normally kill outside the rules of engagement; but superior officers sometimes commanded such breaks with protocol to desensitize soldiers. A soldier goes berserk when he falls into a state of uncontrolled rage in which he is indifferent to his own survival or anyone else's. Going berserk was actually encouraged by officers in Vietnam who did not either know or care that it was a psychological breakdown; instead, they saw it as a useful tactic that made a soldier fearless. All these techniques have only made the moral injury of modern warfare more damaging.

RECENT VETERANS

Accounts of moral injury flow in very readily from recent veterans' combat experiences. Even the responsibility of handling human remains can cause deep moral injury. In her autobiographical book, *Shade It Black,* Jessica Goodell takes readers through her time in Iraq as a Marine in a Mortuary Affairs unit. She and her fellow Marines picked up and cared for the remains of soldiers, many of whom had been all but obliterated by improvised explosive devices. The deployment had an incredibly negative effect on her entire unit. Loss of appetite and insomnia were the milder consequences. Hallucinations and feelings of being haunted by the dead were worse alternatives.

In a May 2017 issue of *Guideposts* magazine, retired Army Sergeant Marshall Powell, who served as a practical nurse in Mosul, tells of the moral injury he struggles with to this day. As the noncommissioned officer in charge of the ICU (intensive care unit) in a combat hospital in Iraq, Powell will never forget the day when at least thirty civilian casualties of a bomb were rushed into his ICU. A tiny little girl was one of the worst casualties, and he knew immediately that she wasn't going to make it. Her agony was so apparent that Powell gave her an overdose of morphine, a decision that haunted him for years. She died painlessly, but later, Powell felt deep shame and guilt and even felt that God could not forgive him for taking her life into his own hands.

Powell was trying to do the right thing in terrible circumstances. Such a soldier may feel like God cannot forgive him for what he has done. But the Church knows otherwise.

A SOLDIER'S TRUST IN JESUS

In some ways, soldiers and others who are affected by moral injury are no different from anyone else. They need Jesus just as any other person does. However, in other ways, such people do bear deep and specific scars, and Jesus cares about those. Jesus does not reject people because of the baggage they carry from life experiences. Rather, He welcomes them. In the Gospels of Matthew and Luke, when a centurion asked Jesus for help in a situation that was out of the centurion's control, Jesus was overjoyed and amazed at the centurion's willingness to trust Him.

> When He [Jesus] had entered Capernaum, a centurion came forward to Him, appeal-
> ing to Him, "Lord, my servant is lying paralyzed at home, suffering terribly." And He
> said to him, "I will come and heal him." But the centurion replied, "Lord, I am not
> worthy to have You come under my roof, but only say the word, and my servant will
> be healed. For I too am a man under authority, with soldiers under me. And I say to
> one, 'Go,' and he goes, and to another 'Come,' and he comes, and to my servant, 'Do
> this,' and he does it." When Jesus heard this, He marveled and said to those who fol-
> lowed Him, "Truly, I tell you, with no one in Israel have I found such faith." . . . And
> to the centurion Jesus said, "Go; let it be done for you as you have believed." And the
> servant was healed at that very moment. (Matthew 8:5–10, 13)

The Holy Spirit enabled the centurion to recognize Jesus' power, liken-
ing Jesus' power and authority to the centurion's own as a Roman officer.
Certainly the centurion's hands were not clean. His job as a leader in the
Gentile Roman army would have required him to do numerous gruesome
and morally questionable deeds. However, Jesus in no way turns away
from him. And what we see in this centurion is one who—despite all of the
authority he possessed, despite the respect he had won in order to become
a centurion—saw in Jesus an authority that gave hope and wholeness in a
way that surpassed earthly authority.

As Jesus was hanging on the cross, there was another centurion, one who
stood facing Jesus. "When the centurion . . . saw that in this way He breathed
His last, he said, 'Truly this man was the Son of God!'" (Mark 15:39). The
centurion at Jesus' crucifixion saw the unnatural darkness from noon to
3 p.m. He experienced the earthquake when Jesus died. Even though the
Roman army was crucifying this man, the centurion saw in Jesus a power
and authority that outlasted the military power under which the centurion
was serving.

After Jesus' death and resurrection, as the early believers in Jesus were
sharing what they had seen and heard, the apostle Peter was sent by God
to the house of Cornelius, a centurion in the Italian Cohort who was also a
God-fearing man—a Gentile who believed in the God of the Old Testament.
As Peter shared the Gospel with Cornelius and all of the people gathered
in his home,

> The Holy Spirit fell on all who heard the word. And the believers from among the cir-
> cumcised who had come with Peter were amazed, because the gift of the Holy Spirit
> was poured out even on the Gentiles. . . . Then Peter declared, "Can anyone withhold

water for baptizing these people, who have received the Holy Spirit just as we have?"
And he commanded them to be baptized in the name of Jesus Christ. (Acts 10:44–48)

Cornelius and his entire household believed in Jesus and were baptized in Jesus' name when they heard who Jesus was and what God had done through Him, giving "forgiveness of sins through His name" (Acts 10:43). Just like the other two centurions we have mentioned, when Cornelius encountered Jesus, he saw in Jesus one who had an authority and a mission much greater than the earthly one Cornelius was a part of as a soldier. By God's grace, the Holy Spirit gave Cornelius faith to trust in Jesus and become a part of Jesus' mission, which gave even greater meaning and purpose to Cornelius's life than his mission as a soldier did.

Not all the soldiers we meet in the New Testament believed in Jesus, but the witness of some of the soldiers who encountered Jesus during His earthly life and who encountered the risen Jesus in the Early Church points us to the wholeness and security that Jesus offers people who have been harmed by moral injury.

READING FOR THE WEEK

Read Psalm 103 and consider how these words help us trust God's mercy and love for us.

DISCUSSION QUESTIONS

1. How might we witness to a serviceperson who doesn't know Jesus but who is seeking answers for the moral injury he or she encountered while serving in the armed forces? What Scripture would you turn to in your witness?

   ....

   ....

   ....

2. Why might military imagery be used to describe God and the work of those who serve in His kingdom in passages like Exodus 14:14; Deuteronomy 1:30; 20:1–4; Joshua 1:5; 1 Samuel 17:45; 2 Samuel 6:2; 7:8–11; Psalm 24:10; 46:7; 84:3; Isaiah 2:12–18; 1 Corinthians 9:7; 2 Timothy 2:3–4?

   ....

   ....

   ....

Lesson 4

WOMEN AND WAR

This week we especially consider the effects of moral injury on women in the military and other women who have suffered abuse or violence.

MILITARY SEXUAL TRAUMA

According to a VA website (www.ptsd.va.gov),[1] about 1 percent of the United States population is in the military. Among that 1 percent, nearly 15 percent is made up of women. Approximately one in five military women report "yes" when screened for military sexual trauma by the Veterans Health Administration. Despite the high virtue ethic instilled in servicepeople during training, there are predators who thrive in military life. The fishbowl that is military culture is not without sharks.

---

1   Other statistics about military servicemen and women can be found at the frequently updated website www.brite.edu/programs/soul-repair/resources/.

Although this section of our study focuses on women, it should be noted that men are not immune to military sexual trauma. Men report "yes" when screened for military sexual trauma by the VA in only slightly smaller numbers than women, and these numbers are only estimates because men tend to report sexual crimes less frequently than women. Either way, sexual violence can cause PTS and moral injury just as easily as combat or other forms of violence, and is as damaging to the person who relives such memories later.

DISTURBING FACTS TO CONSIDER

Hypertension, PTS, and depression are the three most common diagnoses given to women veterans. Couple that statistic with the Pentagon's estimate that 10 percent of women are raped while serving in the military, and we have a high probability that servicewomen returning to civilian and church life bear not only psychological and physical wounds but also moral injury.

VA programs provide health care to nearly 150,000 homeless veterans. One factor that contributes to disproportionately high numbers of veterans among the general homeless population is that it can be difficult for a veteran to hold a job and be focused in the present when his past is so alive in his mind. According to the National Alliance to End Homelessness, female veterans are more likely than male veterans to become homeless, especially women who have served in Afghanistan or Iraq.

Finally, we come to the worst statistic involving female veterans. The latest government research reveals that women veterans commit suicide at a rate six times higher than women who have not served in the military. Part of the reason for this higher rate of successful suicide attempts is that women veterans are more likely to use a firearm to commit suicide than their civilian counterparts.

In previous generations, children of veterans grew up with fathers dealing with the myriad of emotions and symptoms we've seen in both PTS and moral injury. Now, there is a new generation of military children growing up with mothers suffering intensely from these scars. In Lesson 5, we will see how trauma and moral injury can have a residual effect from one generation to the next.

JUDGES 19: AN HONEST VIEW OF HUMAN BROKENNESS

The Bible is actually more honest about the pain and trauma of violence done to women than we may realize. One of the most disturbing and sobering examples of this is in Judges 19, which narrates the most brutal scene in the entirety of Scripture.

The chapter begins with a woman leaving her husband and returning to her father's house. Some English translations call the woman a "concubine," but the Hebrew word is more accurately translated "secondary wife." Secondary wives had certain benefits including that their children were considered legitimate and that they had the means and opportunity to return to their father's house. The text says this woman left her husband because she was unfaithful to him. But we do not necessarily know that she was an adulteress; desertion also qualified as unfaithfulness in the Old Testament.

Four months later, her husband, a Levite, traveled from the hill country of Ephraim to her father's house in Judah to woo her back. His courtship was successful, and she agreed to return to Ephraim with him. But when they set out on their journey a few days later, they left late enough in the day that they had to stay overnight somewhere.

They did not stay in the non-Israelite town of Jebus because the husband thought it would be dangerous to be among foreigners overnight. He expected they would be safer in Gibeah, an Israelite town in the territory of the tribe of Benjamin. When they entered Gibeah, they met an old man returning from the field who offered them a place to stay.

What followed is reminiscent of the account of Sodom and Gomorrah in Genesis but without intervening angels. As the Levite and his wife enjoyed the hospitality of their Gibeahite host, the "men of the city, worthless fellows" surrounded the house and demanded that the host give them the Levite that they might "know him" (Judges 19:22). The host begged the men of the city to take the host's daughter and the Levite's wife instead. When the men refused, the Levite pushed his wife out of the house into the hands of the men who raped her all night. No one came to her aid.

When morning came, the group of men left, and she collapsed at the door of the house where her husband was, with her hands on the threshold. Her husband came out of the house, saw her lying there, and said, "Get up." When she didn't answer, he put her on his donkey, returned home, and then, shockingly, dismembered her body into twelve pieces. He then sent a piece of her body to each of the tribes of Israel as a witness to what had happened. All the people of Israel convened to hear the story of this tragedy.

The Levite was successful in stirring up outrage against the Benjamites. However, the sin in Judges 19 was only compounded by the Israelites' response in Judges 20–21.

The Response: Judges 20–21

What the men of Gibeah did to the woman in Judges 19 was atrocious and sinful. We see that even the rest of the Israelites at the time of Judges condemned these actions as appalling. Yet the response from the Israelites compounded the sin by violently creating another disaster that harmed even more women as well as children.

When the leaders of the tribes of Israel heard the Levite's story, they confronted the tribe of Benjamin. They demanded that the guilty men be brought forward and put to death. The tribe of Benjamin, however, refused to give up any of their men. And with that, the first civil war in Israel began. It ended with the near annihilation of the tribe of Benjamin, leaving only six hundred men left alive.

Before the civil war, the men of Israel had vowed not to let any of their daughters marry the defeated survivors of Benjamin (see Judges 21:1). This posed a problem: one of the twelve tribes of Israel might become extinct. To resolve this problem, the chiefs of Israel sent twelve thousand men to attack Jabesh-gilead, an Israelite town that had refused to fight in the civil war. They killed every male in the town and all of the married women. They took the remaining four hundred girls that had never been married and gave these women to the Benjamite men. Since they were still two hundred women short, they preyed on another group of Israelites who had done nothing! When the virgin daughters of Shiloh celebrated a holy day, they were kidnapped and forced, like the daughters of Jabesh-gilead, to be rape-brides for the remaining Benjamites. The horrific story of Judges 19 that began with violent sexual assault ended in Judges 21 in the same way, only on a much grander scale and sanctioned by the entire nation of Israel.

The Perversity of Sin

What brought about all of this? The author of Judges says the dysfunction in this story and in the rest of Judges comes because at that time in Israel's history, "Everyone did what was right in his own eyes" (Judges 21:25). Indeed, we never hear of the people of Israel asking God how they should handle the situation in Judges 19–21. Instead, they take matters into their own hands, nearly destroy one of the twelve tribes, slaughter almost everyone in another Israelite town, and kidnap and force marriage on hundreds of very young women, possibly some still in childhood.

This series of chapters is a case study of just how perverse and twisted sin is. The Bible is painfully honest about how dark the sin is that lives within us that can commit such horrible actions against others. The Bible is not blind to moral injury of the severest and most terrible kind, including moral injury that particularly takes advantage of women. When we realize that this kind of depravity is possible inside any one of us, we realize how much we need God's forgiveness and grace, given to us because of Jesus' death in our place and the regenerating work of the Holy Spirit to fight our sinful nature.

In an amazing glimpse of redemption, we find out later in the Bible that Saul, the first king God anointed for His people, came from the tribe of Benjamin and was a descendant of one of the kidnapped young women. We do not always see retribution or redemption of evil that is committed. But when Jesus returns, He will at last set all things right.

READING FOR THE WEEK

Read Isaiah 54. In this chapter, God addresses His people as if they are a woman who has been shamed. Note the language of comfort, healing, and redemption as you read this text. Additionally, if you are able, watch the documentary *The Invisible War* (2012) to further understand the moral injury and PTS produced by military sexual trauma.

DISCUSSION QUESTIONS

1. After reading Judges 19–21, what are some examples of moral injury on a national scale that you can think of?

   ----

2. The reckless oath of the Israelites in Judges 21 caused them to behave ruthlessly. Can you recall other rash oaths and oath makers in the Bible? What were the results of their actions?

   ----

3. Scholars and Bible readers have remarked upon the similarities between Judges 19 and Genesis 19 when Lot escaped from Sodom with his daughters. The similarities indicate that by the Judges period, Israelites themselves had grown as cruel and sinful as the Sodomites. Yet, God's judgment did not fall upon Israel for their many sins until many generations later when the Assyrians and Babylonians destroyed the nations of Israel and Judah. How does this comparison of Israel with Sodom make you feel?

Lesson 5

FAMILY AND WAR

This week we will consider the effects of trauma on families. Over the course of decades, major research has been conducted on what is called multigenerational or intergenerational trauma. This research stemmed from serving and caring for Holocaust survivors and their families. Today, these studies shed light not only on the aftereffects of trauma for the survivors but also on the aftereffects for the children and even grandchildren of survivors.

Attachment theory has helped child and family psychologists describe how trauma can affect even later generations who did not experience a trauma firsthand. In the next few pages, we will see how this theory can aid our understanding of this phenomenon, and then we will consider how the Church can come alongside families who are affected in this way.

COPING STYLES AND ATTACHMENT THEORY

Psychologists have identified four typical styles of coping among trauma survivors. People tend to respond either by becoming (a) numb, (b) a victim, (c) a fighter, or (d) a success—someone who makes it through to a normal existence again. The post-traumatic effects that survivors experience naturally affect the way they raise and respond to their offspring. Frequently, the trauma is unintentionally passed on to the children either through overexposure to the parent's traumatic past or through complete silence about the trauma. Consider the WWII veterans who hardly said anything for most of their lives about their war experiences. Many did not open up until after *Saving Private Ryan* appeared in movie theaters. When a trauma is completely shut up by a parent, the communication and bonding between a parent and child is often stilted by the secret that significantly, but silently, influences the parent, whether he or she acknowledges it or not.

Some trauma survivors who are parents become unable to care for the emotional needs of their children. A survivor of a genocide might be distant from and cold to his or her young child, perhaps as a defense mechanism against future hurt. (They may think, "All my loved ones were killed. I can't bear to love that way again.") If that continues, the young child will grow up to be an adult who cannot emotionally relate to his or own spouse and children. Attachment theory shows that bonding patterns are so fundamental and innate to a person they can cause lifelong difficulties when they are not formed healthfully. Since we learn our bonding patterns from our parents or whoever raises us, harmful bonding patterns are very easily handed down from generation to generation.

THE CHURCH'S ROLE

This is a realm in which the Church can truly care for the spiritual needs of an entire family. First, a congregation can provide pastoral care to any and all members of a family through listening and empathy. Love and attention to people goes a long way to introducing them to the love of their heavenly Father, who still offers them the possibility of a secure attachment with Himself.

Second, a congregation's involvement with a family through communal worship and fellowship gives the family a safe place to belong. Becoming a part of a larger community can mitigate the distress of dysfunctional relationships within the family unit. The Holy Spirit's work among bodies of believers allows congregations to be larger families in which immediate families can find support and care when they need a community to lean on.

Third, spiritual direction and ministry through Absolution from ordained pastors help release family members from guilt felt for past relational problems and sins. This gives a family—as well as an individual—the chance to grieve and mourn for the past and then to look forward in hope, knowing that one's life and future are hidden and secure with Christ.

Fourth, what the Church teaches concerning suffering can be a breath of fresh air to families bearing moral injury. The Bible teaches that all suffering is a result of the brokenness of humanity and creation because of sin and our sinful nature. Sin is not a popular concept in our culture, but if we're honest, the idea of "missing the mark" rings true in our lives and experiences. Our fallen, sinful nature causes us inherently to turn in on ourselves, making it possible for people to become perpetrators of abuse against others. The Church speaks the truth about human nature, our lack of goodness on our own, and God's solution—the only real solution—to cycles of abuse and hurt.

The most common family suffering from moral injury in our churches may not be a military family but rather a family suffering from less obvious and yet unaddressed moral injury. For instance, when a woman who had an abortion in her youth marries, she may keep this secret even from her spouse. The sin remains a deep spiritual wound with power over her because it is kept hidden.[2] Domestic abuse creates similarly silent moral injury. Children in particular too often remain silent about physical or sexual abuse in order to protect a parent or family member they love. We can pray for those suffering from silent moral injury in our church and community even as we do our best to make our church a haven of truth, grace, and freedom in Christ for those suffering from moral injury.

TO THE THIRD AND FOURTH GENERATION

God's Word makes it very clear that we as individuals are not islands. No matter our specific responsibilities and specific vocations, the Bible depicts our lives as being very interconnected with those around us. Scripture especially notes this connectedness and the powerful effect one generation can have on another within families. Yet any members within a community can have a similar influence on one another.

God fervently urged His people to be careful to teach to their children all that He had spoken to them. God wanted each generation of His people to know Him and to walk in the way that He said was good (see Deuteronomy 6:1–3, 6–9, 20–25). It was parents' privilege and responsibility to pass along to their children this way of life and this relationship with the Lord. The seriousness of parents' failure to lead their children in the right way by example as well as instruction is why God says the members of a third and fourth generation will experience the aftermath of the sins of the current

---

2   Abby Johnson in her book *Unplanned* gives deep insight into how God can work through moral injury to lead us to healing in Jesus Christ. Her book shares her remarkable journey from being a high-ranking employee of Planned Parenthood to being an outspoken decrier of abortion.

generation (see Exodus 20:5–6). It is not that God is unfair, punishing some people for other people's sins. Rather, most often, subsequent generations follow in the direction that previous generations led.

During His ministry on earth, Jesus urged parents, adults, and caregivers, "Let the little children come to Me and do not hinder them, for to such belongs the kingdom of heaven" (Matthew 19:14). Parents, caregivers, and adults have enormous ability to influence children's relationship with Jesus by whether they lead children toward Jesus or away from Him.

A third example of how intergenerational relationships play a powerful role in a person's formation is what the apostle Paul says about the upbringing of a young man, Timothy, who became one of Paul's fellow missionaries and a leader in the Early Church. Paul was deeply encouraged by Timothy's faith. Timothy was a young man (see 1 Timothy 4:12), and yet Paul was able to write, "I am reminded of your sincere faith, a faith that dwelt first in your grandmother Lois and your mother Eunice and now, I am sure, dwells in you as well" (2 Timothy 1:5).

What the Bible indicates about the importance of one generation's relationship with another shows us the enormous opportunity we have to pass along to the children in our midst the greatest inheritance we could give: a life of faith in Jesus. The importance of intergenerational relationships is also sobering as we realize the potential damage we can do if we ignore the moral injury in our lives and in our communities.

READING FOR THE WEEK

Read Psalm 17. Contemplate what it reveals about God's mercy and heart for those who have been abused and violated, as discussed in the previous two weeks' lessons.

DISCUSSION QUESTIONS

1. Describe the spiritual influence your parents had on you.

2. How has the role of your parents in your faith life impacted the way you share the Good News of Jesus Christ with your children and grandchildren?

3. What examples do you see in the Bible of the cry of the innocent victim for God's help?

Lesson 6

TWO OLD TESTAMENT EXAMPLES

In this lesson, we will bridge the previous five lessons' description of moral injury to the next six lessons' focus on how God speaks into situations of moral injury. In this lesson, we consider two examples of moral injury in the Old Testament and notice how God spoke into those situations. Both examples surround the destruction of the nation of Judah in the 500s BC.

JEREMIAH: THE ULTIMATE OUTSIDER

Jeremiah began to prophesy during the reign of King Josiah, a king of Judah who desired to follow God. However, the message God gave to Jeremiah was one that many of the people and later kings of Judah did not want to hear. It was Jeremiah's job to say that tragedy and destruction were coming if the kings and the people of Judah did not turn from the way they were going and turn to follow God's ways. But the response to Jeremiah's message was not at all what he had hoped for or expected.

Jeremiah reached a point in his ministry when the burden of his calling felt too heavy. He didn't want to be God's prophet anymore. He felt betrayed by his fellow people who refused to listen to God. But more than anything, Jeremiah felt betrayed by the Lord Himself. In this way, Jeremiah's experience bears the mark of moral injury. Moral injury can happen when someone feels he has been betrayed by someone in authority, someone in whom he trusted and relied. Jeremiah was so upset at one point, he cried out:

> O LORD, You have deceived me, and I was deceived; You are stronger than I, and You have prevailed. I have become a laughingstock all the day; everyone mocks me. For whenever I speak, I cry out, I shout, "Violence and destruction!" For the word of the LORD has become for me a reproach and derision all day long. If I say, "I will not mention Him, or speak any more in His name," there is in my heart as it were a burning fire shut up in my bones, and I am weary with holding it in, and I cannot. (Jeremiah 20:7–9)

His misery over the people's response was so great he tried to avoid further disappointment by simply not saying the things God had given him to prophesy. Yet he could not refrain from speaking. There was a burning fire inside him that compelled him to speak. Finally, he was so miserable that he cursed the day he was born, wishing instead that his mother had died with him in childbirth (see Jeremiah 20:14–18).

Jeremiah was so miserable because he felt God had betrayed him by giving him an impossible task. Why did God call him to be a prophet if the people were not going to listen? The price Jeremiah paid for being God's prophet was being threatened repeatedly, put in stocks, lowered into a cistern, starved, almost killed by a mob, nearly killed by a king, plotted against, and beaten. No wonder he was miserable. The situation did not get much better at the end of his life. Eventually, he was forced by a stubborn remnant of people from Judah to go to Egypt against his will and against God's command. We don't know exactly how Jeremiah's life ended, but Jewish tradition says he was stoned to death by Israelites in Egypt who were exasperated at his preaching.

Few of us would envy Jeremiah's sufferings. Yet, how God responded to Jeremiah's moral injury tells us something about how He responds to our moral injury. Jeremiah's story illustrates that no matter how wounded, traumatized, or angry we are, even at God, God will not forsake us. Even though Jeremiah accused God of deceiving him, God promised that He would not abandon Jeremiah and that He would take care of him (see Jeremiah 15:16, 19–21).

Jeremiah's story also reflects how God can work good even in the midst of pain. Although the call of being God's prophet was so costly for Jeremiah, God still worked faithfully through him to reveal to God's people why they were sent into exile, to give them the opportunity to repent, and to pave the way for them to see their need for redemption and forgiveness, won by Jesus on the cross.

THE CAPTIVITY PSALMS

The same event that Jeremiah prophesied about is also involved in our second example of moral injury in the Old Testament for this week's lesson. However, it is the national moral injury that we will look at this time.

The destruction of Jerusalem and the temple in 587 BC was the annihilation of the Judahites' world and an event that created a devastating moral injury for the nation. It is hard for us, in the luxurious security we enjoy as Americans, to conceptualize what the people of Judah went through when the Babylonians subjugated them. But Scripture gives us a glimpse of the level of their national moral injury in what are called "the captivity psalms."

Psalm 74 vividly describes the destruction of the temple by the Babylonians. In it, we hear the shock of a people who had thought God would never allow this to happen to His holy place. The idea had been inconceivable.

Psalm 137 is hard to hear because its severity makes us wonder how God could allow this psalm to be in the Scriptures. Yet what we hear in the intensity of this psalm is how deeply the experience of being sent into exile was scarred into the Israelites' corporate memory. Something so devastating would not easily leave the people's national identity.

EZEKIEL: HOPE IN CAPTIVITY

Ezekiel was the prophet to God's people while they were in the captivity that these psalms depict. Although the language in the Book of Ezekiel is graphic and perhaps even disturbing at times, we have to understand that the people he was talking to had been emasculated and deeply traumatized by what they had brought upon themselves. They had been violently removed from their country. The men could not stop their women from being enslaved or their babies from being killed. Families and lives had been torn apart. Ezekiel gave voice to this in sometimes extremely violent and sexual imagery. He and the people were in shock. God called Ezekiel to start to help his fellow captives understand why God had allowed this to happen. Through Ezekiel, God revealed to His people that He was not present in Jerusalem when the Babylonians destroyed the city. Ezekiel described how the glory of God had already abandoned the temple before the Babylonians came because the people were worshiping other gods (see Ezekiel 8:1–11:13).

He also explained that God had not been captured or defeated by the Babylonians when Jerusalem fell. Instead, God promised His people that even in spite of their unfaithfulness that brought this national tragedy, He was in control of the rising and falling of nations. Through Ezekiel, God not only instructed His people how to make sense of their destruction and exile. God also gave them a deep and living hope in His mercy. He promised to remain with them in their captivity. He promised that He would give them a new heart and a new spirit (see Ezekiel 11:14–25). He promised that He would raise up for them a new shepherd (see Ezekiel 34). And He promised that there was a future, a new life for His people. "My dwelling place shall be with them; and I will be their God, and they shall be My people" (Ezekiel 37:27).

The last recorded prophesy in the Book of Ezekiel is a vision of the new Israel and new Jerusalem that God will bring about one day. The prophet in exile ends by proclaiming, "The name of the city from that time on shall be, The Lord Is There" (Ezekiel 48:35). Through Ezekiel, God says there is a hope and a future for even a nation suffering from moral injury. It is a secure hope grounded in God's mercy.

READING FOR THE WEEK

Read Psalm 74 this week in light of this lesson.

DISCUSSION QUESTIONS

1. Why do you think Jeremiah and Ezekiel may have suffered moral injury?

   _____

   _____

   _____

2. Have you ever felt angry at God, perhaps during the darkest moments of your life? What do you make of Jeremiah's complaints against God?

   _____

   _____

   _____

Lesson 7

A LESSON IN LAMENTATION

From this week forward, we look at different approaches to the care and healing of the spirit. This week we start with what healing can come through lamentation, using Jesus' response to His sufferings as a guide.

The most important thing we could ever say about the cross is that Jesus won there our salvation, removing the power of our sins over us and paying for our sins by His substitutionary death in our place.

But for the victim of moral injury, it is striking to note that God's means of healing and restoring us was to send His own Son into our flesh to experience an extreme moral injury on our behalf. But Jesus did not just endure great moral injury—He saved us through His moral injury. And for us He triumphed over moral injury's ultimate power. He is our light and comfort even in our darkest periods of suffering. Because He is our Savior, He also teaches us how to pray and how to suffer by His own example and through God's Word. If He lamented through a suffering far greater than any that will fall upon us, He can comfort and sustain us through our sufferings.

AN ANCIENT SPIRITUAL PRACTICE

The ancient spiritual practice of lamentation was prevalent in the Old and New Testaments but has been all but forgotten in the contemporary Western Church.

Biblical lament in the Early Church guided a Christian through his suffering. It was not something that a person did once and never practiced again. Rather, it was something a person could and should use throughout a lifetime and for many different reasons. It is based in Jesus' own lamentation while He hung on the cross. He cried out, "My God, My God, why have You forsaken Me?" (Matthew 27:46). Jesus did not ignore or cover over the agony He experienced when He was abandoned and forsaken on the cross by His heavenly Father. In the same way, we, as God's children, are invited to cry out to Him, rather than to try to ignore our pain. In fact, God's Word testifies that bringing our complaints to God is the best place to take them.

The Psalms are often used in the practice of lamentation because there are many lamentations already built into the Psalms. In fact, 40 percent of the Psalms are laments.

THE FIVE PARTS OF A LAMENT

Lamenting is not simply venting; rather, it is a highly structured form of speech. It is composed of five parts.

No. 1—The Address

The first part of the lament is the address to God. It is usually a simple, "My God!" or "O Lord!"

The name by which we address God relates to the particular lament we are expressing. In the Garden of Gethsemane, Jesus called out, "*Abba*, Father." *Abba* is an intimate way to address one's father, a term of endearment similar to our English "Daddy." When we address God as "Almighty God," we are bringing to mind God's all-encompassing power over our lives, our world, and everything we experience. When we address Him as "Eternal Lord," we are encouraged that, because God has no beginning and no end, He outlasts everything else we experience, and that He gives us a share in His eternal life through Jesus.

No. 2—The Complaint

Next, the lamenter brings before God the cause of his or her (or someone else's) suffering. The complaint can be anything: ill health, pain, disappointment, depression, enemies, false accusations, abandonment, betrayal, loss, tragedy. Nothing is out of bounds.

Because we approach God in an intimate relationship, there is no need to hold anything back. It can be terrifying to face painful memories and overwhelming emotions that we try to shut off and lock deep inside. Yet, when Jesus prayed in the Garden of Gethsemane, He did not try to hide His emotions or thoughts from His Father. Jesus teaches us to face our overpowering emotions in prayer. God promises He will be with us and will carry us through, no matter how painful the burdens are that we bear. He loves us and cares so deeply for us; He wants to hear our honest complaints.

No. 3—The Request

The complaint is then followed by a petition. This is a request for help, asking God to see to a need.

The request reorients the sufferer. The sufferer asks God to create and give a different situation than the one he or she is currently in. Therefore, the request allows the sufferer to hope. Biblical hope is not simply wishful thinking. Instead it is an absolutely sure confidence in the healing and restoration Jesus Christ will bring when He returns on Judgment Day. God in His mercy gives us hope, and the Holy Spirit helps us trust God's promises. We do not invent our own hope. But hope powerfully brings meaning back into our lives.

No. 4—The Promise

The psalms of lament usually also mention promises that God has already made, asking Him to remember and carry out His promise. This recounting of God's promises and praying them back to Him gives the sufferer confidence that God is "our refuge and strength, a very present help in trouble" (Psalm 46:1).

No. 5—Expression of Praise

The reminder of God's promise gives us reason to praise God, even when we are suffering. In the last section of a lament, the lamenter shifts from expressions of suffering to expressions of confidence. The praise that ends a lament also helps lead the sufferer out of the darkness into a new situation that is focused on the Redeemer. This element shows how Scripture can change the attitude of our heart and allow for God's regenerative Spirit to work something new within us—peace, hope, even joy.

CHRIST'S PRESENCE WITH US

As an illustration of how Jesus is with us in the midst of our laments, consider Mary Magdalene's perception of Jesus' presence on Easter morning. When Jesus was crucified, His disciples were dumbfounded and shocked. Everything they had hoped in was lost. They were utterly devastated. If there was ever a time for lamentation, it was this one.

In John's Gospel, Mary Magdalene went early on Sunday morning to the tomb where Jesus had been laid. It was still dark when she arrived, but she discovered that the tomb had been opened and Jesus' body was missing. To her, it seemed that someone had stolen Jesus' body, only compounding and intensifying the grief of those who were mourning His death. She stood outside the tomb weeping.

When she looked in the tomb again, she saw two angels sitting where Jesus' body had been. They asked her why she was crying, and she told them how she was convinced that Jesus had been taken away. Suddenly she turned around, and Jesus was standing right behind her. But she did not recognize Him. Jesus asked her why she was weeping, and she told Him. But it was not until Jesus spoke her name that Mary realized that the Jesus she thought she would never see again was right there with her.

Until Jesus comes back, we do not get to see Him face-to-face. Yet, as for Mary at the tomb, Jesus is with us, even when we doubt His presence and even though we can't see Him face-to-face now. He calls us by name in our Baptism, and we hear His voice in His Word while we wait for Him to return. What He tells us in His Word is that He is with us even when we are not sure that He is. He is with us when we cry out to God in a lament. He is with us in the midst of our sufferings. And His promises invite us to lament our suffering, even as His promises invite us to trust Him.

READING FOR THE WEEK

Read some of the psalms of lament. See if you can identify the five elements of a lament that we discussed in this lesson. Here are some of the psalms of lament: 3, 4, 5, 7, 10, 13, 17, 22, 25, 26, 28, 31, 39, 41, 42, 43, 53, 54, 55, 56, 57, 59, 61, 64, 70, 71, 77, 86, 120, 139, 141, 142.

DISCUSSION QUESTIONS

1. Psalm 34:18 tells us that God is near to the brokenhearted. The Bible also tells us that God hears the blood of the innocent who are slain crying out to Him (see Genesis 4:10; Hebrews 12:24; Revelation 6:10). With this in mind, what do you think about the spiritual practice of lamenting? Is the idea of lamenting foreign to you, or is it similar to your own prayers during troubling times?

2. Have you ever considered what the time between Good Friday and Easter Sunday was like for Jesus' disciples? What emotions might they have had that mirror the emotional responses we have to moral injury? After experiencing those emotions, what would they have felt when they saw the resurrected Jesus?

3. The Protestant poet John Donne wrote devotional sonnets[3] for the purpose of focusing the mind, quelling distractions, and enabling a person to pay attention in prayer. Reading the sonnet closely, line by line, focuses the reader's attention upon God so that by the end of the preparation, the reader can begin her own conversation with God with a less distracted mind. This week when you come before God in prayer, read the following poem-prayer by Donne and consider how Jesus' resurrection changes everything—including the power of death over us.

---

3   If you are interested, John Donne's collection *Holy Sonnets* is in public domain and available online.

DEATH, BE NOT PROUD
BY JOHN DONNE

Death, be not proud, though some have called thee

Mighty and dreadful, for thou art not so;

For those whom thou think'st thou dost overthrow

Die not, poor Death, nor yet canst thou kill me.

From rest and sleep, which but thy pictures be,

Much pleasure; then from thee much more must flow,

And soonest our best men with thee do go,

Rest of their bones, and soul's delivery.

Thou art slave to fate, chance, kings, and desperate men,

And dost with poison, war, and sickness dwell,

And poppy or charms can make us sleep as well

And better than thy stroke; why swell'st thou then?

One short sleep past, we wake eternally

And death shall be no more; Death, thou shalt die.

Lesson 8

JESUS HEALS US

The Presence, Touch, and Word of Jesus

In the previous lesson, we studied the biblical lament as a guide for working through our sufferings. In this lesson, we consider three of the ways Jesus heals us.

GRACE

In the Bible, the Greek word *charis* can mean simply "a gift or favor," but it also specifically refers to God's undeserved love. This is the first way Jesus heals us. Whenever God reveals Himself to us or comes to us, He is giving us His grace. He is initiating a relationship with us that we could never create or find on our own. The greatest outpouring of God's grace was when He allowed His Son to die on the cross in our place. Every time we receive Jesus, whether in hearing God's Word or in receiving the Sacraments, God heals us with His grace—He forgives us and brings us back into His family.

Jesus' Grace to Peter

Peter was one of Jesus' twelve disciples, one of His closest friends. Peter had been present through all of Jesus' ministry. Peter's devotion to Jesus seemed evident when Jesus foretold that all twelve disciples would fall away from Him, and Peter declared, "Though they all fall away because of You, I will never fall away" (Matthew 26:33). He even went so far as to say, "Even if I must die with You, I will not deny You!" (Matthew 26:35). Yet, when Jesus was arrested and on trial before the high priest, Peter betrayed Jesus and did the exact opposite of what he had promised.

> Simon Peter followed Jesus, and so did another disciple. Since that disciple was known to the high priest, he entered with Jesus into the courtyard of the high priest, but Peter stood outside at the door. So the other disciple, who was known to the high priest, went out and spoke to the servant girl who kept watch at the door, and brought Peter in. The servant girl at the door said to Peter, "You also are not one of this man's disciples, are you?" He said, "I am not." (John 18:15–17)

This question and Peter's response were repeated two more times in that scene. In Mark's account, Peter even invoked a curse on himself and swore that he did not know Jesus. When Peter realized that he had done exactly what Jesus had said he would do—deny Jesus three times before the rooster crowed—Peter wept (see Mark 14:72).

After Jesus rose from the dead, He appeared to His disciples in a number of places and instances. In John 21, Peter and some of the other disciples were fishing on the Sea of Tiberius when suddenly Jesus was standing on the shore, calling to them. He told them to cast their nets on the other side of the boat. They pulled in so many fish that their nets started to break, even though they had caught nothing all night. Jesus then invited them ashore for breakfast.

Jesus had prepared a fire of burning coals, and he was cooking fish over the coals for their breakfast. The Greek word for a coal fire is *anthrakia*. Curiously, the only other time this word is used in the New Testament is in John 18:18, describing the coal fire in the courtyard of the high priest when Peter denied Jesus three times.

Then, in John 21:9, Peter approached that same Jesus and smelled the same scent of burning coals. What happened next? Jesus asked Peter a question—three times. "Do you love Me?"

Jesus lovingly confronted Peter in a way and in circumstances that did not allow him to ignore the sin and pain that were festering in him. Jesus loved Peter enough not to avoid him but rather to confront him and to pour grace over Peter's betrayal. Jesus reinstated Peter and forgave him. Jesus met Peter in exactly the way that was necessary to remove all doubt that Jesus had restored the relationship between them and that Peter's place in the work of God's kingdom was restored. Peter's failure and Jesus' grace in response comfort us enormously and give us hope. Peter's experience shows us just how abundant God's grace is.

REMAINING

In the Upper Room before His death, Jesus told His disciples, "Abide in Me, and I in you. As the branch cannot bear fruit by itself, unless it abides in the vine, neither can you, unless you abide in Me. I am the vine; you are the branches. Whoever abides in Me and I in him, he it is that bears much fruit, for apart from Me you can do nothing" (John 15:4–5).

The metaphor of being connected to a stronger life source than oneself is powerful for the Christian who is a trauma survivor. What exactly does the word *abide* in this text mean? The Greek word could also be translated "remain."

To "remain" does not just mean staying in one place. It can also mean waiting, enduring, or even surviving. It is carried out by remaining in God's Word and continuing to receive God's gifts in Christ's Body, the Church. In some ways, Jesus' teaching that we are to remain in Him is as difficult as any other teaching He gave to us. We may be tempted away from remaining by distractions and pursuits that at times seem more important than Jesus. Others have faced the real possibility of being harmed or killed as the price of remaining in Jesus.

Remaining in Jesus is a life lived between Jesus' promise and the reality we experience right now. Survivors of violence are acutely aware of the difficulty of this. Yet Jesus invites us to remain in Him and with Him because He knows being connected to Him, the true vine, is the best place that we can be.

THE ONE WHO COMES ALONGSIDE

In John 14:15–17, Jesus made a great promise to His followers:

If you love Me, you will keep My commandments. And I will ask the Father, and He will give you another Helper, to be with you forever, even the Spirit of truth, whom the world cannot receive, because it neither sees Him nor knows Him. You know Him, for He dwells with you and will be in you.

Jesus promised that the Father would send a helper to Jesus' disciples. The Greek word translated "Helper" here is *parakletos*; it means "the one who comes alongside." The idea evoked here is of a defender or an advocate—someone who stands beside you during a trial.

The Holy Spirit was given to Jesus' Church at Pentecost, and the Helper has been with those who believe in Jesus ever since. We have an advocate and a defender who comes beside us through our trials. We are never alone when we have been baptized into Jesus. The Helper helps us remain in Jesus; He brings to our remembrance all that Jesus has said to us in His Word (see John 14:26). He delivers Jesus' grace to us and gives us faith through God's Means of Grace: Baptism, Holy Communion, the Word, and Confession and Absolution. Jesus heals us by His Holy Spirit—the Comforter, who binds us to Jesus and gives us all good things in Him.

READING FOR THE WEEK

Read chapters 14, 15, and 21 in the Gospel of John.

DISCUSSION QUESTIONS

1. What does remaining in Jesus look like?

2. How is the Holy Spirit described by Scripture?

3. In the previous lessons, we have often discussed moral injury as something that happens to us. Yet in Peter, we can see that we can inflict spiritual damage on ourselves. What part does grace play in healing damage to the soul?

Lesson 9

PAUL

Treasure in Jars of Clay

God used the apostle Paul in a powerful way in the Early Church. He was one of the most influential first missionaries. He wrote thirteen of the twenty-seven books in the New Testament. Yet, Paul at one time seemed like the most unlikely candidate to be a primary spokesman for the Church. His past haunted him throughout his life. And yet positively, his past continually reminded him all he had to offer to others was only what God had graciously and abundantly given to him.

Paul was a descendant of the tribe of Benjamin (see Philippians 3:5). He received a high-quality religious education and was trained as a Pharisee, with thorough religious discipline and piety. Paul's zeal for his Jewish faith was so strong he became a notorious persecutor of the Christian sect, viewing them as a heretical offshoot of the Jewish religion. Paul infamously participated in the stoning of the first Christian martyr, Stephen. "The witnesses laid down their garments at the feet of a young man named Saul" (Acts 7:58).

Paul was so convinced that Christianity was a dangerous cult that needed to be stamped out, that he went to the high priest in Jerusalem and got permission to go to synagogues in Damascus and bring to Jerusalem any people in those synagogues who believed Jesus was the Messiah and He had risen from the dead. Yet on the way, Paul's life changed forever in a way he never would have expected. As he described in Acts 22,

> As I was on my way and drew near to Damascus, about noon a great light from heaven suddenly shone around me. And I fell to the ground and heard a voice saying to me, "Saul, Saul, why are you persecuting Me?" And I answered, "Who are You, Lord?" And He said to me, "I am Jesus of Nazareth, whom you are persecuting." (Acts 22:6–8)

This shocking confrontation with the risen Jesus created a cataclysmic shift for everything in Paul's life. Jesus had confronted him in a way he was not able to ignore or deny. A man as serious and obedient as Paul felt a sense of horror when he realized how wrong he had been about who Jesus was. The zeal and conviction he had in following the God of Abraham, Isaac, and Jacob now was applied to fully and completely trusting Jesus, God's Son, and to carrying out Jesus' mission.

PAUL'S MINISTRY

Jesus told Ananias, whom God sent to interpret for Paul what had happened while Paul was on the road to Damascus, "He [Paul] is a chosen instrument of Mine to carry My name before the Gentiles and kings and the children of Israel. For I will show him how much he must suffer for the sake of My name" (Acts 9:15–16). Paul became every bit as determined to spread the Gospel as he previously had been to stamp it out. Yet, in spite of how hard he worked, how passionate he was about the grace and love of God given in Jesus, how much he suffered for his confession of faith, Paul never forgot what he had done in his former life. He considered himself "the least of the apostles, unworthy to be called an apostle, because I persecuted the church of God" (1 Corinthians 15:9).

The guilt Paul carried over what he had done to Christians and to the Lord Jesus through those persecutions of the Church was a burden much like moral injury that lingered in Paul's life. How was he able, nevertheless, to become the greatest Christian missionary ever?

JARS OF CLAY

Paul proclaimed consistently and faithfully that there was nothing in him that made his ministry and mission what it was. He wrote, "I will boast all the more gladly of my weaknesses, so that the power of Christ may rest upon me" (2 Corinthians 12:9). He claimed only to have "this ministry by the mercy of God" (2 Corinthians 4:1). Concerning his own role in the work of God's kingdom, Paul said, "We have this treasure [the Gospel of Jesus] in jars of clay, to show that the surpassing power belongs to God and not to us" (2 Corinthians 4:7). God chose an unlikely emissary to proclaim His Word and demonstrate His power. Yet in Paul's life, we see that God's grace is sufficient (see 2 Corinthians 12:9) to use any one of us, no matter what moral injury we may carry. Just like Paul, our own scars do not make us unsuitable for God to use as He sees fit within His kingdom.

God is more than capable of using imperfect people to work in the lives of others. Just because we have suffered moral injury ourselves does not mean God cannot still work through us to care for others who are suffering from moral injury. Still, addressing our own wounds and moral injury is very important. God cares about our well-being as well as others'. He wants us to seek help and healing. As we heal, we, too, then have treasures in jars of clay: God's love and grace given abundantly to us, which we can then share with others. For "the surpassing power belongs to God . . . not to us" (2 Corinthians 4:7).

READING FOR THE WEEK

Read 2 Corinthians 1:1–11.

DISCUSSION QUESTIONS

1. What are the advantages and disadvantages of having religious fervor or zeal?

   _____

   _____

   _____

2. It has been said that all Christians are like Paul—converted persecutors. In what ways can you relate to Paul?

   _____

   _____

   _____

Lesson 10

CHRIST IN THE POW CAMP

In this lesson and the next, we look at the experiences of two individuals who suffered moral injury in the twentieth century and testify to the power of Jesus' victory in the midst of moral injury.

JÜRGEN MOLTMANN'S STORY

Jürgen Moltmann is a well-known theologian, but his experience is also an example of how moral injury can shape a life for the better—indeed, how it can lead one to the light of God's love.[4]

Moltmann grew up without a religious education; he was raised in a tiny German farming commune during the rise of the Third Reich. Moltmann was required to participate in Hitler Youth camps. In 1943, he and the other

---

4   The content about Jürgen Moltmann in this chapter can be found in his book *A Broad Place: An Autobiography* (Minneapolis: Fortress Press, 2009).

boys in his school class were conscripted as air force auxiliaries and stationed in Hamburg.

On July 24, 1943, more than one thousand British aircraft rained down explosive and incendiary bombs over Hamburg. A bomb hit a platform where Moltmann was standing next to his good friend. Miraculously, Moltmann was left virtually untouched, but his friend was instantly torn apart. For the first time, Moltmann asked God, "Where are You?" He also struggled with survivor's guilt.

Months later, Moltmann was visited by his father, now a major in the German army, who revealed a haunting secret. He had discovered that the Jews of Minsk, where he was serving, had been mass murdered and buried in mass graves. This secret broke Moltmann's will to serve his country. He bitterly believed the war's continuing efforts were merely a cover-up for the crimes committed against the Jews. His father also suffered intense moral conflict, which went unresolved for many years.

In 1944, Moltmann was eighteen years old and was called up to serve in an infantry battalion. Again he witnessed a close comrade die and questioned why he was spared. In his first real skirmish with the British, he surrendered and was sent to a POW camp in Belgium.

When the war ended in 1945, he was transported to Camp 22 in Kilmarnock, Scotland, and a chaplain there gave him his first Bible. Reading through that Bible and experiencing the unrelenting kindness of the Scottish villagers, Moltmann began to encounter Jesus. When he read Jesus' words on the cross—"My God, why have You forsaken Me?"—Moltmann began to believe Jesus Christ was the only one who could ever understand him or know his suffering. Meeting Christ in the POW camp was unexpected and life-changing for him.

During his time in the Scottish camp, Moltmann noticed that German soldiers who did not have faith in Jesus fared much worse than their believing counterparts. There was an utter lack of hope among these men that led them to despair. When they saw Allied photos of the Jewish survivors of concentration camps, many German prisoners were devastatingly ashamed of their participation in their country's national crimes against humanity. Many never wanted to return home; others did not want to go on living. Moltmann himself at times lost his will to live.

THREE FACTORS IN SUICIDE

Moltmann's despair and his observations about other soldiers' despair can help us understand in a very real way how some who are suffering from moral injury are attracted to suicide. One theory proposes the following three factors increase the possibility someone may choose suicide:

1. Feeling that one doesn't belong

2. Feeling that one is a burden to others

3. Overcoming the fear of pain and harm

The first two factors—feeling socially isolated and alienated—can create the third factor. Such feelings can become so all-encompassing they overpower the natural tendency to avoid harming oneself. This can be true of a teenage boy as much as it can be true for an eighty-two-year-old veteran. Even if a veteran becomes a civilian, marries, and creates a seemingly "normal" life, unaddressed shame from his or her experiences often still dwells underneath everything else. The elderly and widowed who also suffer from moral injury can be doubly susceptible to feelings of isolation and guilt from the past. The combination of such factors can lead to suicide.

The suicide of Colonel Ted Westhusing, a West Point professor of philosophy, English, and ethics, while he served in Iraq in 2005 was one event that helped spur the U.S. military to acknowledge that moral injury exists. Westhusing seemingly had everything to live for: a family, a very successful military career, and a Christian faith. Yet his suicide note described despair from seeing his convictions betrayed in Iraq. This shocked military commanders into reassessing their methods and questioning why clinical approaches to despair can fall short.

Psychologists who study suicide have found that the most effective way to help prevent it is to blunt the isolation at whatever cost. Just being physically, mentally, and emotionally present in the same house or room with someone suffering from moral injury can be enough to help carry a person through battles with despair, even without saying anything.

DEEP LISTENING

One of the ways that we can be like the Scottish villagers in Moltmann's story and blunt the isolation of those suffering from moral injury is to truly listen to a morally injured person. This can deeply help a person process his or her trauma. Processing memories is an important step in healing. Individuals and congregations can promote healing by developing the practice of an empathetic kind of listening known as deep listening.

Facts about Listening

Research studies conducted by the International Listening Association shows that we spend about 45 percent of our time listening to others. We are distracted or forget the things we hear 75 percent of that time that we listen to others. Since an adult's average attention span is twenty-two seconds, we can usually only remember about half of the things someone says to us right after he or she speaks to us. After a few hours, we remember only 20 percent of what we heard.

Clearly, deep, attentive listening does not come naturally to most of us. It is an ability we must cultivate and practice. In a way, deep listening is like prayer—it requires focus and attention.

Some Principles for Practicing Deep Listening

There are a few principles that can help us work toward mastering the art of deep listening. First, listen to understand, *not* to judge, evaluate, or try to fix someone. Understanding involves trying to comprehend where the speaker is in life and how the events she relays are affecting her.

Second, don't speak unless you are sure the speaker wants a response. When you do speak, speak authentically, from your heart. This can be difficult because it requires being open and vulnerable yourself.

Third, respect the speaker's trust that caused him to open up to you and share his thoughts, feelings, or experiences with you. Always ask if you are able to share his story with others or if he wants you to just keep it to yourself. If you repeat without his permission what was shared with you, even in the form of a prayer request, you will destroy the person's trust and could potentially cause him further moral injury.

Fourth, be truly present when you are listening to someone else. Don't be distracted by your own thoughts, plans, assumptions, skepticism, or desire to respond. As a culture, we are not comfortable with silence. We want to fill moments of silence as quickly as possible to avoid the discomfort we feel. But interrupting silent moments can effectively signal that you are trying to take over the conversation, that you are a speaker now not a listener, and that the other person no longer has the opportunity to say whatever he wants to, however and whenever he wants to.

LESSONS ON HOPE

When Jürgen Moltmann was released from the POW camp in Scotland, he returned to Germany and was drawn to theological studies. Moltmann became known as a theologian of hope. He focused on the hope of all Christian believers: the return of Jesus Christ and the resurrection of the dead. During a sermon fifty years after he was released from the POW camp at an event for former POWs, Moltmann quoted Psalm 30:11–12, a psalm of thanksgiving:

> You have turned for me my mourning into dancing;
> > You have loosed my sackcloth and clothed me with gladness,
> that my glory may sing Your praise and not be silent.
> > O LORD my God, I will give thanks to You forever!

Through the kindness of the Christians he encountered in the POW camps, Moltmann came to trust God's promises. He found in Jesus a hope that was able to make him thankful, in spite of all that he had been through and experienced. He had hope because God promised that one day, all things will be made new. Resurrected believers will have bodies that will no longer decay and die, and they will share in eternal fellowship and perfect union with their Creator and King. This is the beautiful promise of Isaiah 2:2–4:

> It shall come to pass in the latter days that the mountain of the house of the LORD shall be established as the highest of the mountains, and shall be lifted up above the hills; and all the nations shall flow to it, and many peoples shall come, and say: "Come, let us go up to the mountain of the LORD, to the house of the God of Jacob, that He may teach us His ways and that we may walk in His paths." For out of Zion shall go forth the law, and the word of the LORD from Jerusalem. He shall judge between the nations, and shall decide disputes for many peoples; and they shall beat their swords into plowshares, and their spears into pruning hooks; nation shall not lift up sword against nation, neither shall they learn war anymore.

READING FOR THE WEEK

For this week, read Psalm 39; Mark 15:1–41; and Psalm 30. Try to read them through the eyes of someone like the young Moltmann.

DISCUSSION QUESTIONS

1. What do you think of the idea of blunting or breaking isolation?
   Have you ever been present for someone in this way before?

   ----

2. In his autobiography, Moltmann emphasizes the kindness of the
   Scottish people. They treated him like their neighbor and not like
   their enemy. If you were in a similar situation, do you think you
   would be able to respond like the Scottish people?

Lesson 11

CHRIST IN THE
INTERROGATION CHAMBER

Trauma survivors wrestle with the memory of the event(s) that changed their worldview forever. In this second-to-last lesson, we consider memory one last time. To do this, we will walk with our final guide, a pastor and theologian named Miroslav Volf.[5] His story will help us understand not only how the past can haunt someone but also how our ultimate destination in history is the consummated kingdom of God.

---

5   The content about Miroslav Volf in this chapter can be found in his book *The End of Memory: Remembering Rightly in a Violent World* (Grand Rapids: Eerdmans, 2006).

MIROSLAV VOLF'S STORY

In 1984, Volf was a PhD candidate at a school in the West. However, since he was a citizen of what was then Yugoslavia, he was obligated to return home to fulfill a required year of military service. He knew he would be under close scrutiny by the communist government and his military superiors because he was the son of a Protestant pastor, he was married to an American woman, he was writing a dissertation on Karl Marx (who had different views on socialism than the Yugoslavian government), and most of all, he was a Christian.

Volf knew the chances of trouble with the government were high, but he underestimated his situation. For the first few months on the military base, he was unaware his entire unit had been ordered to spy on him. They struck up seemingly innocuous conversations with him about his Bible, beliefs, politics, or ethnic identity. Unknown to him, all these conversations were reported to his officers.

Soon many "conversations" with his captain began. A foot-thick file on his captain's desk held transcripts of Volf's conversations with his wife and translations of his letters. Volf's psychological torture began, and it continued throughout his year of military service.

Interrogation after interrogation followed. New interrogators came and went, but his captain was always present, always questioning. Charges were followed with threats. Since he was in the military, he was told he would face a closed military tribunal without an independent lawyer to defend him. He was told he would likely spend at least eight years in prison for his "crimes" against the state.

Volf was at the mercy of his captain and interrogators. He felt helpless—no way to go, and no one to turn to for justice. Although he was never physically tortured, the fear of what his captors could do was relentless and paralyzing. They were all-powerful and all-seeing; Volf could do nothing.

REMEMBERING

When his year of military service ended, Volf returned to his life. Though his interrogation torture abruptly ended, his mental torment did not. An unwanted presence had entered his mind—the captain. Volf's mind was violated, and he couldn't get the violator out. How could he ever trust again?

As he moved into a career in theology, Volf was troubled by what to do with the memory of his abuse. As a Christian, he was taught to forgive and to love his neighbor and to pray for his enemies. Volf slowly realized he had to learn how to remember rightly in order to be able to do that.

FORGIVENESS AND REMEMBERING

Jesus on Forgiveness

"If you do not forgive others their trespasses, neither will your Father forgive your trespasses" (Matthew 6:15). Jesus' words can be a difficult pill to swallow.

When dealing with moral injury, it is crucial to remember that on the cross, Jesus paid not only for our sins against God but also for our sins against one another. (After all, sins we commit against others are always sins against God too.) Since Jesus already paid for the wrong in the trauma committed against me, I have no right to refuse to forgive the sinner who committed it. That being so, we must look at how we choose to remember events and to think about the party who wronged us.

The Spiritual Discipline of Attending

One way to lay our memories before God is in prayer. Paul wrote, "Rejoice always, pray without ceasing, give thanks in all circumstances; for this is the will of God in Christ Jesus for you" (1 Thessalonians 5:16–18). Paul exhorts us to pray without ceasing in *all* circumstances. Yet for most of us, prayer is difficult; our attention is often scattered. Why is talking to God so hard?

Man's fall into sin made him naturally opposed to God, rather than in union with Him. But even when we are reconciled to God through Christ, our fallen nature causes us to struggle to pay attention and focus on even our daily tasks and work, much less on the gift of prayer to our transcendent Creator. How much harder it is, then, for someone who suffers from PTS symptoms or moral injury to pray since such a person's body is in hyperalert survival mode.

The spiritual discipline of attending can be helpful for us and especially for the person suffering from moral injury as preparation for prayer. It is like getting one's mind and body to "stand to attention" in the presence of God before we begin communicating with Him. The English word "attend" comes from the Latin word *attendere*. It includes the idea of stretching toward something. Attending is practiced by meditating on a Scripture passage, psalm, or devotional poem in a slow and deliberate fashion until one's heart and mind are calmed and focused. The words used for the attending exercise are not especially important. What is important is only that the words do not add to one's distraction. It is appropriate to repeat phrases or words as needed until one is able to focus on them. That is a signal that one is ready to begin prayer. English cleric Thomas Becon called this the lifting up of the mind. This exercise can also prepare us to hear and read God's Word, which slowly heals us and opens us up to eventually forgive as Jesus has forgiven.

REMEMBERING TRUTHFULLY

Can we control how we recall our past? Miroslav Volf began to explore this idea and what memory means for the Christian. According to Volf, it does matter how we remember a wrongdoing and how we tell our stories of that memory. Does the remembering allow us to harbor a grudge? Do we only allow ourselves to recall the worst in the person who has hurt us and never any good memories? Do we exaggerate a person's actions against us in our remembering and retelling, or do we attribute motives to their actions beyond what we can know?

Volf realized telling his story was important for his healing. If a memory is never told, it is like a fresh scar that continues to burn and never heals or fades. The injured person needs to talk about what happened to be able to put the trauma in perspective. A person cannot look forward to the joyful moments God gives when her worst memory still has a death grip over her life.

But Volf also advocated that we must learn to remember rightly when we have been hurt by others. Remembering rightly is being as honest as possible when we remember and vocalize our abuse. We do not need to hold back or make excuses for a perpetrator. However, we also do not need to exaggerate the wrongdoing. Volf considered Martin Luther's discussion of the Eighth Commandment, "You shall not give false testimony against your neighbor," in the Large Catechism. Luther described how the Eighth Commandment calls us to protect the honor and reputation of our neighbors by covering over their sins. Covering over their sins does not mean downplaying their sin or pretending it doesn't matter to God; rather, it means protecting another person's reputation and forgiving him or her. Trying to get back at a perpetrator by slandering him or her is an act of vengeance, not justice.

Yet, this doesn't mean that honestly acknowledging that we have been wronged and hurt qualifies as bearing false witness. The Eighth Commandment forbids going *beyond* a true witness, in both our memory and our public telling of the story. We are exhorted to speak truth *in love*. The motivation for speaking is being a conduit of God's grace to our neighbor by the freedom that comes through hearing and speaking the truth. Since the meaning we attach to memories is determined over time by how we remember, we must practice remembering rightly, so that we might outwardly speak truth in love.

OUR FRAMEWORK FOR MEMORIES

In order to remember rightly and truthfully, we need a framework within which our memories can be addressed and placed. This framework is crucial for healing and forgiveness. Without it, we have only a collection of damaging memories that continue to wound and haunt us.

In the story of God's redemption of the world through His Son, Jesus, we have a framework within which to place our memories. Jesus' willingness to accept suffering, pain, and even death to win us as His very own is in our corporate memory. Every time we partake of the Lord's Supper, we remember His solidarity with us in undergoing the pain we feel in this world. Even more than that, every time we partake of the Lord's Supper, we remember that Jesus has taken the sin of all wrongdoers—including us—on Himself. We taste and eat and drink the evidence that we were once enemies of God, but we were reconciled to God through Jesus' unconditional love for us and now are called God's sons and daughters (see Romans 5:6–11).

REDEMPTION AND NONREMEMBRANCE

Volf advocated the idea that eventually being able to forget a wrongdoing is a gift from God—the beautiful gift of nonremembrance. How is this possible, we might ask, when a memory is so horribly seared into one's mind? Nonremembrance is putting something out of one's mind. The prophet Isaiah described how God does this when He chooses to no longer remember His people's transgression from the past: "For behold, I create new heavens and a new earth, and the former things shall not be remembered or come into mind" (Isaiah 65:17).

Christians for centuries have wrestled with how we can practice this nonremembrance and mirror God's covering over our sin. The apostle Peter, for example, wrote, "Above all, keep loving one another earnestly, since love covers a multitude of sins" (1 Peter 4:8).

Yet, nonremembrance is only something that we can pray for and receive as a gift from God. Many of us receive only glimpses of this gift while we are still in this fallen world. Even if we never reach a point when we can truly forget a wrong done to us, an ultimate removal of painful memories is one of the promises in store for our redemption. There will be a day when God will make all things new and set all things right. Then He will relieve the burden of all the memories of wrongs and sufferings that we carry.

Some believe that to forget is to allow for injustice; but when God tells us to forgive, He is promising that we do not need to hold on to our hurts because, in the end, He will sort it all out. He is foreshadowing for us the day when "He will wipe away every tear from their eyes, and death shall be no more, neither shall there be mourning, nor crying, nor pain anymore, for the former things have passed away" (Revelation 21:4).

READING FOR THE WEEK

Read Isaiah 43:16–25. Do a word study on *forget* in the Bible, and see if you can find other Bible passages that speak of nonremembrance.

DISCUSSION QUESTIONS

1. Miroslav Volf linked the idea of memory with Luther's discussion of bearing false witness. Do you think this is too far of a stretch, or do you agree with Volf that we can remember wrongly or rightly?

   _____

   _____

   _____

2. Have you ever heard someone claim that there are some wrongs they could never forgive? Have you ever felt this way personally? Considering Volf's insight into memory, nonremembrance, and the kingdom of God, has your view changed at all? What would you say to someone who says they can never forgive in light of Jesus' words, "If you do not forgive others their trespasses, neither will your Father forgive your trespasses" (Matthew 6:15)?

   _____

   _____

   _____

3. What do you think of Jesus' command to forgive those who sin against us seventy-seven times? How does forgiveness bear witness about the world that is to come?

   _____

   _____

   _____

Lesson 12

WHERE WE GO FROM HERE

I n this concluding lesson, we will consider some ways your local congregation can relate to people who suffer from moral injury. We will look at several types of ministries and services that churches can implement to help serve veterans, military personnel, and others who have survived violent trauma.

THE ROLE OF THE CHURCH

Our local churches are uniquely equipped to help the morally injured. However, like the public at large, many Christians are very uninformed about the issues we have discussed in this study. Many veterans who reenter civilian life end up avoiding their home churches because they feel they can't relate to other members and that they don't belong within the fellowship anymore.

Veterans do *not* want to be viewed as victims. Nor do they want to be viewed as heroes. Many feel that they have done dishonorable or at least questionable acts during their time in service to our nation. If the Church approaches veterans in either of these two ways, they will see through it and likely walk away from the Church.

The Church needs to understand that some veterans feel intense guilt for acts that they have perpetrated against others as representatives of our country. These men and women have been our society's protectors, and they want to continue to be productive in our society. But addressing their PTS and/or moral injury is a must before they can fully reintegrate into society.

The Church needs to be a safe place to express anger. Those with moral injury are usually very angry: at God, at themselves, and at the world. When we in the Church are confronted by anger, we often default to seeing that anger as sin, and by saying as much to the person, we inadvertently shame the person who is angry. Comments like "You should never be angry at God!" distract from the goal of helping a person deal with the root cause of his or her anger and discourage any further discussion. Anger covers up grief, and if churches do not allow the morally injured to work through their anger, the grief underneath cannot be addressed in the community of the Body of Christ and true healing cannot take place. Remember, there are plenty of examples of people in the Bible who believed in God and yet simultaneously directed their anger toward Him: Gideon, David, Job, and Jeremiah.

DEEP LISTENING

We have discussed in earlier lessons just how important deep listening is and how congregations are filled with people who can have a Christlike presence for those who need to speak about their experiences. When it comes to veterans, there are certain dos and don'ts that pertain to any conversation:

Don't ask inappropriate questions that can cause further moral injury, such as "How many people did you kill?"; "What was it like to kill someone?"; "Who was the first person you killed and what did they look like?"

Do ask questions like "Are there any memories from that time that still bother you?"; "Did you sense the presence of God during this time?"; "How are you doing now?"; Do you have a sense of purpose?"

Do be respectful and nonjudgmental.

Do expect intense answers.

Do be knowledgeable of resources within the church and your community.

Don't try to "fix" a veteran or tell them that "it's okay." Just listen to their story so that they can put the past into perspective. The Spirit of God will work internally on their heart. Your part is to be still and listen.

RESOURCES AND RITUALS

The Church already has liturgical rituals and practices for dealing with grief; so a church's ministerial staff can tap into these traditions on significant days of the year like Memorial Day and Veterans Day. Such opportunities can help individuals express grief through the comfort of corporate lamentation. There is more that your local church can do, though. Please consider the following resources and ministries that your congregation could pursue in caring for those suffering from moral injury.

H.E.R.O.E.S. CARE

H.E.R.O.E.S. stands for Homefront Enabling Relationships, Opportunities, and Empowerment through Support. This is a nongovernmental organization. Such organizations are approved by the VA to provide services to veterans and their families in communities across the country. H.E.R.O.E.S. Care partners with churches through Stephen Ministries. If your church is already involved in Stephen Ministries or has congregants who are, you should seriously consider contacting this organization. At an appointed time every week during a deployment and the following two years, a volunteer calls a serviceperson who is enrolled with H.E.R.O.E.S. The volunteer is committed to that serviceperson (always of the same gender) and present for him or her throughout this time in his or her life. For further information, go to:

heroescare.org/about/heroes-care/

heroescare.org/partners/stephen-ministries/

COMFORT DOG MINISTRIES AND KARE 9 MILITARY MINISTRY

These nonprofit organizations train dogs and their handlers to bring mercy, comfort, and the presence of Christ to hospitals and to victims of disasters. Kare 9 specifically brings the care of Comfort Dogs to veteran hospitals, homes, and living centers. Currently, there are twenty-four states that have at least one Comfort Dog, and this nonprofit is growing. If your church is interested in becoming a home for a Comfort Dog and training handlers, go to:

www.lutheranchurchcharities.org/k-9-ministries1.html

OPERATION BARNABAS

This program was created by The Lutheran Church—Missouri Synod's Ministry to the Armed Forces to provide care for chaplains and their families, to train congregations to support and care for military personnel and families in their communities, and to provide resources to other similar organizations who support those connected with the military. Operation Barnabas is especially interested in working with organizations like local chambers of commerce, schools, and medical facilities who can help returning servicepeople rejoin their civilian communities. For more information, go to:

www.lcms.org/ministry-to-the-armed-forces/operation-barnabas

QUILTS OF HONOR

There are several organizations that quilt or knit blankets for veterans or military servicepeople. The quilter may never get to meet the soldier or veteran who will receive the blanket, but the quilter can connect to the recipient of the quilt by praying for that unknown person while creating the gift. For more information, go to:

quiltsofhonor.org/

ADULT SUNDAY SCHOOL ON LAMENTATION

One simple and natural way to instill compassion for those who suffer moral injury is to teach a class on the spiritual discipline of lamentation. This discipline enables Christians to know how to meet with God during times of tragedy and grief. Pastors can build up a body of believers who know how to lament and who are spiritually bolstered for the dark times when they come. If there is a pattern of prayer that the congregation is already familiar with, corporate lamentation can be integrated into that when the church grieves together as a body.

GROUP MEETINGS

Your church buildings and facilities can be a blessing to your overall community. You could let a veterans' group meet regularly in one of your rooms or buildings. You could also help organize off-site groups, such as fly-fishing groups, swimming groups, equine groups, or adventure sport groups, in which veterans from the church can do activities together and form close relationships in the process.

Your church could form an anonymous, off-site group for women who have suffered moral injury through abortions. It is best if the location of the group's meetings is not disclosed to those in the church who are not a part of the group so that there is confidentiality for those involved. Someone trained in pastoral care or counseling would need to facilitate the gatherings and be the contact person for those interested in joining the group.

TENSION AND TRAUMA RELEASE EXERCISES

TRE, or Tension and Trauma Release Exercises, are simple exercises developed to help those with PTS symptoms. These exercises encourage the body to return to a natural state, to calm the nervous system, and to allow for physiological healing. These exercises can be done individually or in groups. To watch a video and learn more, go to:

traumaprevention.com/what-is-tre/

THE SOUL REPAIR CENTER

This think tank and education center focuses on moral injury. The website shares multiple resources, congregational aids and materials, and other organizations that a congregation can partner with. For more information, go to:

brite.edu/programs/soul-repair/about_soul_repair/whatwedo/

LAST WORD

When the leper pleaded, "Lord, if You will, You can make me clean" (Matthew 8:2), Jesus' response was simple. In the original language, He said one word that meant "I want" or "I desire." God *wants* to heal us; He *wants* to bind up our broken hearts, heal our spiritual brokenness, give rest to our souls, and bring us near to Himself. As He draws us near to Himself, may He also make us willing participants in His work of mending others' moral injury.

DISCUSSION QUESTIONS

1. Now that the study is coming to an end, what are your thoughts and perceptions about moral injury?

2. Is there an organization or ministry that you know of that could be included in our list as a church resource? Please share your knowledge with your church.

LEADER GUIDE

To the instructor: In the last section of every lesson, you will find a recommended Scripture reading for the week. Begin and end every class with a prayer. There is suggested prayer material for the beginning of class at the start of each lesson, or you can create or find other prayers that fit the themes.

LESSON 1: CRISIS OF CONSCIENCE

To the instructor: The opening prayer for this week is Lamentations 3:17–24. You can involve the class in the prayer by reading the text responsively, dividing the text into "leader" and "group" parts, and providing the Bible text for the class. You can also use sensory experiences to help participants focus while listening if only you read the text. You can light a candle, sound a gong, or play a short recording of instrumental music.

1. **Can you think of anyone in your personal history who was touched by moral injury?**

   This is a chance for your class to discuss their understanding of moral injury. If you need an icebreaker, try to relay to your class an example from your life. For instance, I used the story of my grandfather who was an Army paratrooper during WWII and a POW twice. I explained how his return home from war affected his family. With no way to address his "shell shock," or moral injury in the form of survivor's guilt, he self-medicated and became an abusive alcoholic. This had a major impact on how his children turned out and how I was raised. Alternatively, you could also read statements from victims of mass shootings or bombings as examples.

2. **Who else besides those who have witnessed or participated in combat and warfare could be at risk for spiritual trauma caused by violence?**

   Police officers, EMTs, firefighters, doctors, nurses, pilots, journalists, lawyers, counselors, and crime-scene photographers are all some possible answers.

3. **Why do you think the rise of scientific knowledge undermined the general belief in humans' spiritual nature?**

   As Western society rose out of the Middle Ages, it relied on science and the scientific method to help answer all of life's questions; consequently, there was also a rejection of metaphysical things like superstition, mysticism, and religion. Remember, science can only study that which is observable. Therefore, truth, beauty, love, and the human spirit cannot be observed this way!

4. **What does it mean to be an image-bearer of God? In other words, what qualities do we as human beings exhibit in our nature that reflect our Creator?**

   Answers might include our creativity, our sense of eternity, our ability to love, and so on.

LESSON 2: BODY AND SOUL

To the instructor: The opening prayer for this week is Psalm 7.

1. **In the lesson, memory is described with the metaphor of a jigsaw puzzle. What are some other ways to conceptualize how memory works?**

   Others have used the imagery of a patchwork quilt or Lego building blocks. This is a chance for your class to creatively consider different ways to envision memory.

2. **What is the difference between PTS and moral injury? What symptoms do they share?**

   PTS is physically observable with brain scans; a physical change happens in the brain after a trauma. Moral injury is spiritual trauma, identifiable through a person's emotions. See the table that shows the differences and similarities between the symptoms of the two kinds of injury.

3. Read Deuteronomy 4:1–4, 9–10; Matthew 11:28–30; Hebrews 4:11–13 concerning what the Bible says about our heart, soul, and spirit. How do these verses affect your understanding of human nature?

> Deuteronomy 4 reminds us of the importance of keeping and holding God's words and His works in our heart. Matthew 11 contains Jesus' promise to carry our burdens and give us His light and easy yoke, which provides rest for our souls. He points out His gentle and lowly heart. Hebrews 4 reminds us that God's Word exposes the thoughts and intentions of our hearts and can even divide the thin line between our spirit and our soul. Therefore, God cares deeply about our soul, spirit, and heart.

4. Moral behavior is developed first through imitating parents and caregivers. Why do you think Paul emphasized imitation in 1 Corinthians 4:16; 11:1; and Philippians 3:17?

> Imitation is key in discipleship. We can see Scripture complementing what we now know to be scientific fact. Human beings are imitation machines! Jesus gives us the ultimate example to imitate, showing us what it means to be a true human being before God.

LESSON 3: THE FATHERS VS. FREUD

To the instructor: The opening prayer for this week is Psalm 103.

1. How might we witness to a serviceperson who doesn't know Jesus but who is seeking answers for the moral injury he or she encountered while serving in the armed forces? What Scripture would you turn to in your witness?

> This is a very subjective question. The point is to introduce such a person to Scripture that might speak to them personally. The penitential psalms and the Scriptures we've mentioned above are all possibilities.

2. Why might military imagery be used to describe God and the work of those who serve in His kingdom in passages like Exodus 14:14; Deuteronomy 1:30; 20:1–4; Joshua 1:5; 1 Samuel 17:45; 2 Samuel 6:2; 7:8–11; Psalm 24:10; 46:7; 84:3; Isaiah 2:12–18; 1 Corinthians 9:7; 2 Timothy 2:3–4?

> In the Old Testament, God is said to fight for His people. This is an amazing source of comfort because that means Israel's protection and well-being does not depend on how strong and powerful they are. In fact, God says He purposefully picked Israel as His nation because they were the smallest and weakest nation on the earth. In their weakness, God's strength is seen even more fully. God is also often referred to as "the LORD of hosts" in the Old Testament. A host is a military term that means "army." Therefore, this title is usually used in contexts where God's role as the leader of angelic armies and of the armies of Israel is relevant. He is the true leader of His people who will fight to defend His name among them, no matter what earthly leaders they may have. Paul uses the imagery of being a soldier in service to Christ to evoke the devotion and commitment that he and his fellow workers have toward Jesus and the mission of God's kingdom.

LESSON 4: WOMEN AND WAR

To the instructor: Opening prayer is Isaiah 54:1–6. This week's lesson is likely going to be the most difficult one that your class will read. When I taught this segment to a large class of older adults and seniors, several people wept, and a few came to me afterward to tell me their stories. So be prepared for the potential difficulty of this week.

1. After reading Judges 19–21, what are some examples of moral injury on a national scale that you can think of?

> Responses in my class included the aftermath of the Civil War, racial division in the U.S. due to slavery and Jim Crow, the plight of Native Americans, the experiences of Holocaust survivors, and the experiences of the Japanese people after Hiroshima and Nagasaki.

2. The reckless oath of the Israelites in Judges 21 caused them to behave ruthlessly. Can you recall other rash oaths and oath makers in the Bible? What were the results of their actions?

> Jephthah's oath in Judges 11:29–40; Saul's vow in 1 Samuel 14:24–46.

3. Scholars and Bible readers have remarked upon the similarities between Judges 19 and Genesis 19 when Lot escaped from Sodom with his daughters. The similarities indicate that by the Judges period, Israelites themselves had grown as cruel and sinful as the Sodomites. Yet, God's judgment did not fall upon Israel for their many sins until many generations later when the Assyrians and Babylonians destroyed the nations of Israel and Judah. How does this comparison of Israel with Sodom make you feel?

> We love the story of God's salvation history so much that sometimes we put the Israelites on a pedestal or, at the very least, we minimize how much they deserved God's punishment and wrath that they experienced later in their history. Yet, stories that bare their utter sinfulness—like ours—help us appreciate all the more the depth of God's love and mercy in sending His only Son to die on the cross for our sins.

LESSON 5: FAMILY AND WAR

To the instructor: The opening prayer today is from Psalm 102.

1. Describe the spiritual influence your parents had on you.

> Before we look at how we share the Gospel with our children, it is often helpful to think briefly about how our parents impacted us. There is no need for embarrassment here—no one is responsible for how well or poorly he or she was raised.

2. How has the role of your parents in your faith life impacted the way you shared the Good News of Jesus Christ with your children and grandchildren?

> This discussion can help parents recognize strengths and weaknesses they acquired from their parents and consider

what they might do differently for their own children going forward.

3. **What examples do you see in the Bible of the cry of the innocent victim for God's help?**

Answers could include many of the Psalms, Joseph in Genesis, Job, Isaiah's Suffering Servant passage, Jesus on the cross, Stephen in Acts, and so on.

LESSON 6: TWO OLD TESTAMENT EXAMPLES

To the instructor: Opening prayer is Jeremiah 17:14–18.

1. **Why do you think Jeremiah and Ezekiel may have suffered moral injury?**

Jeremiah felt betrayed by both his own people who did not listen to his prophesying and by God who gave him the commission. Those who suffer moral injury often feel betrayed by their superiors and/or by God. Ezekiel personally suffered from the enslavement and captivity he endured. He also saw many of his own people tortured and killed or enslaved.

2. **Have you ever felt angry at God, perhaps during the darkest moments of your life? What do you make of Jeremiah's complaints against God?**

This is a personal question, so individuals' answers will depend on their experiences. You can remind your class that Job and David often demonstrated anger against God and were still counted among God's people. Many times we think that it is not okay to be angry with God, but Scripture reveals that God doesn't stop loving us or working in our lives even if we are honest with Him about what we think and cry out in anger and frustration.

LESSON 7: A LESSON IN LAMENTATION

To the instructor: Use a psalm of lament for the opening prayer. Here is a list of the traditional communal psalms of lament: Psalms 44; 60; 74; 79; 80; 85; 90. Psalms of lament for individuals are listed under the Reading for the Week.

1. **Psalm 34:18 tells us that God is near to the brokenhearted. The Bible also tells us that God hears the blood of the innocent who are slain crying out to Him (see Genesis 4:10; Hebrews 12:24; Revelation 6:10). With this in mind, what do you think about the spiritual practice of lamenting? Is the idea of lamenting foreign to you, or is it similar to your own prayers during troubling times?**

   This is an open-ended question to garner discussion about the spiritual discipline of lament. Many participants may discover that they could benefit from considering God's promises and praising Him after crying out to Him for help. Feel free to share with the class some of your own favorite Scripture passages that encourage you when you are troubled.

2. **Have you ever considered what the time between Good Friday and Easter Sunday was like for Jesus' disciples? What emotions might they have had that mirror the emotional responses we have to moral injury? After experiencing those emotions, what would they have felt when they saw the resurrected Jesus?**

   From the figure in Lesson 2, we know that guilt, anger, shame, sorrow, alienation, and a sense of betrayal can all be emotional responses to moral injury. The emotions the disciples experienced when they realized Jesus had risen from the dead give us a glimpse of what we will feel one day when Jesus comes back and we live with Him forever.

3. **The Protestant poet John Donne wrote devotional sonnets for the purpose of focusing the mind, quelling distractions, and enabling a person to pay attention in prayer. Reading the sonnet closely, line by line, focuses the reader's attention upon God so**

that by the end of the preparation, the reader can begin her own conversation with God with a less distracted mind. This week when you come before God in prayer, read the following poem-prayer by Donne and consider how Jesus' resurrection changes everything—including the power of death over us.

Read "Death, Be Not Proud" by John Donne on page 56.

LESSON 8: JESUS HEALS US

To the instructor: Open in prayer with John 14:18–19.

1. What does remaining in Jesus look like?

When I first taught this class, I was asked what remaining looked like, practically speaking. Remind the class that the primary way of keeping Jesus' commandments is to believe in Him. Loving one another flows from our new relationship with God through faith. This also means we are enabled to confess that we are followers of Christ, even when it is uncomfortable or dangerous to admit it.

2. How is the Holy Spirit described by Scripture?

The Spirit of Truth, the Helper, the Comforter, the Paraclete, the One Who Comes Alongside, the Defender, the Advocate, the Counselor.

3. In the previous lessons, we have often discussed moral injury as something that happens to us. Yet in Peter, we can see that we can inflict spiritual damage on ourselves. What part does grace play in healing damage to the soul?

God's grace moves us to repentance. God forgives us for past sins because He is gracious. God gives us His grace in Absolution. God's grace is a free gift, not something we can work for or make happen. Because Jesus lived a perfect life and suffered an innocent death, we receive God's grace through Jesus. Because of Jesus, grace is something we can ask for in prayer.

LESSON 9: PAUL

To the instructor: Opening prayer is 2 Corinthians 1:1–11.

1. **What are the advantages and disadvantages of having religious fervor or zeal?**

   When zeal is born from our love, honor, and adoration of the Lord, it is a good thing. But when zeal becomes destructive anger or cold narrow-mindedness, our zeal can drive people away from the Lord. It is best to feel our zeal with humility, having a tremendous desire to meet others where they are and to look for opportunities to share our faith in joy and gentleness.

2. **It has been said that all Christians are like Paul—converted persecutors. In what ways can you relate to Paul?**

   This is a very subjective question in order to prompt the class to think about Paul's story, their own story, and how God works through their infirmities.

LESSON 10: CHRIST IN THE POW CAMP

To the instructor: Open in prayer with Psalm 39:9–12.

1. **What do you think of the idea of blunting or breaking isolation? Have you ever been present for someone in this way before?**

   This is an open-ended, group-discussion question about the ideas in this lesson. There really is no wrong or right answer.

2. **In his autobiography, Moltmann emphasizes the kindness of the Scottish people. They treated him like their neighbor and not like their enemy. If you were in a similar situation, do you think you would be able to respond like the Scottish people?**

   Try to help your group imagine a similar circumstance that would affect them. There are people in our own neighborhoods whom we might be tempted to view as "the enemy." Can we extend kindness to them, just as the Scottish did to the German POWs?

LESSON 11: CHRIST IN THE INTERROGATION CHAMBER

To the instructor: Open in prayer with Isaiah 65:17–18.

1. **Miroslav Volf linked the idea of memory with Luther's discussion of bearing false witness. Do you think this is too far of a stretch, or do you agree with Volf that we can remember wrongly or rightly?**

   Jesus indicated in the Sermon on the Mount that commandments are broken inwardly (e.g., lust is the same as adultery) as well as outwardly, so Volf's argument about memory is plausible. Sin begins with the inclinations of the heart, and it is very likely that memory is affected by our hearts' desires.

2. **Have you ever heard someone claim that there are some wrongs they could never forgive? Have you ever felt this way personally? Considering Volf's insight into memory, nonremembrance, and the kingdom of God, has your view changed at all? What would you say to someone who says they can never forgive in light of Jesus' words, "If you do not forgive others their trespasses, neither will your Father forgive your trespasses" (Matthew 6:15)?**

   This is a subjective question meant to prompt the group to discuss their thoughts about this lesson. The hope is also that this lesson and your discussion of it can help participants come to a place where they can forgive, even if they initially say that they can't.

3. **What do you think of Jesus' command to forgive those who sin against us seventy-seven times? How does forgiveness bear witness about the world that is to come?**

   Jesus' ministry shows us what God's kingdom will look like. This is why Jesus healed the paralytic and blind men and forgave them. We know that in the future Kingdom there will be no physical limitations. But with Jesus, healing is always bigger than just physical ailments. Healing is also always equated with forgiveness.

LESSON 12: WHERE WE GO FROM HERE

To the instructor: Open in prayer with Matthew 8:2–3. Since this session is shorter than the previous eleven sessions, I would encourage you to spend some time with your class looking at the list of resources provided and considering which ones your congregation might be interested in and able to pursue.

1. Now that the study is coming to an end, what are your thoughts and perceptions about moral injury?

   Let your group freely share their impression of what they learned.

2. Is there an organization or ministry that you know of that could be included in our list as a church resource? Please share your knowledge with your church.

   There are many ministries that I have not mentioned, some only statewide. This is a time for your group to inform one another on possible ministries that your church can become involved in, within the local community or even nationwide.

Illustrations

FURTHER RESOURCES

Alexander, Caroline, and Lynn Johnson. "Healing Our Soldiers." *National Geographic*. February 2015.

Bellinger, Charles K. *Jesus v. Abortion: They Know Not What They Do*. Eugene, OR: Cascade Books, 2016.

Brock, Rita Nakashima, and Gabriella Lettini. *Soul Repair: Recovering from Moral Injury after War*. Boston: Beacon Press, 2012.

Carey, Greg. "John 21:1–19: Repairing Our Grief." *The Blog. Huffington Post*, June 11, 2013. http://www.huffingtonpost.com/greg-carey/john-211-19-repairing-our-grief_b_3047725.html (accessed November 19, 2017).

Doucet, Marilyn, and Martin Rovers. "Generational Trauma, Attachment, and Spiritual/Religious Interventions." *Journal of Loss and Trauma* 15 (March 2010): 93–105.

Egnor, Michael. "A Map of the Soul." *First Things*, June 29, 2017. https://www.firstthings.com/web-exclusives/2017/06/a-map-of-the-soul (accessed November 19, 2017).

Frankl, Viktor E. *Man's Search for Meaning*. Boston: Beacon Press, 2006.

Gafney, Wil. "Speak! What Judges 19 Has to Say about Domestic Violence." *Sojourners*, October 5, 2015. https://sojo.net/articles/troubling-texts-domestic-violence-bible/speak (accessed November 19, 2017).

Goodell, Jessica, and John Hearn. *Shade It Black: Death and After in Iraq*. Haverton, PA: Casemate Publishers, 2011.

Hall, Elizabeth Lewis. "Suffering in God's Presence: The Role of Lament in Transformation." *Journal of Spiritual Formation and Soul Care* 9 (Fall 2016): 219–32.

Henriksen, Jan-Olav, and Karl Olav Sandnes. *Jesus as Healer: A Gospel for the Body*. Grand Rapids: Eerdmans, 2016.

Jacobs, Janet. *The Holocaust across Generations: Trauma and Its Inheritance among Descendants of Survivors*. New York: New York University Press, 2016.

Johnson, Abby. *Unplanned*. Carol Stream, IL: Tyndale, 2014.

Litz, Brett T., Nathan Stein, Eileen Delaney, Leslie Lebowitz, William P. Nash, Caroline Silva, and Shira Maguen. "Moral Injury and Moral Repair in War Veterans: A Preliminary Model and Intervention Strategy." *Clinical Psychology Review* 29, no. 8 (2009): 695–706.

Marcus, Joel. *Jesus and the Holocaust: Reflections on Suffering and Hope.* New York: Doubleday, 1997.

Marno, Dave. *Death Be Not Proud: The Art of Holy Attention.* Chicago: University of Chicago Press, 2016.

Marshall, Samuel Lyman Atwood. *Men against Fire: The Problem of Battle Combat.* Norman, OK: University of Oklahoma Press, 1947.

Moltmann, Jürgen. *A Broad Place: An Autobiography.* Minneapolis: Fortress Press, 2009.

Moon, Zachary. *Coming Home: Ministry That Matters with Veterans and Military Families.* St. Louis: Chalice Press, 2015.

Powell, Marshall. "The Price of Caring." *Guideposts* (May 2017): 38–43.

Rambo, Shelly. *Spirit and Trauma: A Theology of Remaining.* Louisville: Westminster John Knox Press, 2010.

Sherman, Nancy. *Afterwar: Healing the Moral Wounds of Our Soldiers.* New York: Oxford University Press, 2015.

Shore, Mary Hinkle. "Stand by Me: Memorial Day and the Healing of Souls." *The Blog. Huffington Post*, July 19, 2014. http://www.huffingtonpost.com/mary-hinkle-shore/memorial-day-and-the-healing-of-souls_b_5353012.html (accessed November 19, 2017).

van der Kolk, Bessel. *The Body Keeps the Score: Brain, Mind, and Body in the Healing of Trauma.* New York: Penguin Books, 2014.

Volf, Miroslav. *The End of Memory: Remembering Rightly in a Violent World.* Grand Rapids: Eerdmans, 2006.

Winright, Tobias, and Laurie Johnston, eds. *Can War Be Just in the 21st Century?: Ethicists Engage the Tradition.* Maryknoll, NY: Orbis Books, 2015.